AF481295

Jesus

Jesus

A Story of Love

Adolfo Quezada

Contents

*For my Father, who first
introduced me to the life of Jesus.*

Preface

This book is very personal for me because I consider myself a follower of Jesus. If the word "disciple" means to be a student of, then I am also a disciple of Jesus. I am one of many, and there are probably as many ways to experience the spirit of Jesus as there are disciples of Jesus. God created each of us unique unto ourselves, so the way each of us experiences Jesus is also unique.

Jesus is like a cut diamond that varies its appearance depending on the angle from which it is viewed. Although different, all views are valid. What remains constant in the diamond, regardless of the view taken, is its strength, its beauty, and its preciousness.

I know that Jesus is a historical figure. He lived and died more than two thousand years ago. Yet, the spirit of Jesus lives on in me, and influences my life in every way. My faith in God is based on Jesus' faith in God.

I am so grateful to this man whom I never met, but whose spirit lives within me.

The subtitle of this book is "A Story of Love" because I cannot bring Jesus to mind or to heart without evoking the spirit of love. For me, Jesus and love are synonymous. From the beginning of his ministry to the end, he made love the core of his message.

The Pharisees were constantly debating Jesus, trying to trap him with their questions. One of them, a lawyer, asked him, "Which commandment in the law is the greatest?" Jesus answered him, "'You shall love the Lord your God with all your heart, and with all your soul, and with all your mind.' This is the greatest and first commandment. And a second is like it: 'You shall love your neighbor as yourself.'" (Mt 22:34-40)

For Jesus, love was not only the greatest commandment; It was also the essence of God. He told the lawyer, "On these two commandments hang all the law and the prophets." He could have also added, love is the matrix of life itself.

Introduction

Even as they went about the business of daily living, men and women were abruptly interrupted by the call, "Follow me."

As they looked up from their routine tasks, they beheld a man, a man who stood firm and spoke with conviction. For some reason beyond their comprehension, they were compelled to listen to his words and to follow him.

Jesus of Nazareth, a person much like themselves, called men away from their businesses and their regular lives to become itinerant beggars. He inspired women to follow as well and to share from their own resources. He called men and women away from the concrete and the secure to what he believed to be a greater life – a life dedicated to God.

What pull, what attraction could there have been for those who abandoned their lives as they had known them to follow Jesus so readily? What could he offer them that was worth such upheaval? What was so special about this man?

Some called Jesus a rabbi, but he was very different from the rabbis of his time. As his ministry developed, Jesus taught not only from synagogues, but also in open fields, hillsides, and lakes. Jesus associated with thieves, prostitutes, and even tax collectors. The traditional rabbis of the time would avoid these "socially unacceptable" people.

Was Jesus a prophet? Some called him that, and even Jesus referred to himself as a prophet on occasion. When Jesus was teaching in the synagogue in Nazareth, his hometown, people took offense at him because they knew him as a local resident and wondered where he had learned what he was teaching. Jesus lamented, "Prophets are not without honor except in their own country and in their own house." (Matthew 13:57) After Jesus' death, one of his followers, Cleopas, declared that Jesus was "...a prophet mighty in deed and word before God and all the people." (Luke 24:19)

Was Jesus one of the "scribes," as the teachers of his time were called? Rather than draw from the same academic sources as the scribes did, Jesus' inspiration came from his deep and prolonged communion with God. His intimate connection with God was more like that of the Galilean holy men to whom Jesus had been exposed over three decades of his life. The scribes' teaching, on the other hand, was predominantly founded on the sacred texts.

Jesus had probably studied the Torah (the first five books of the Bible), and showed a familiarity with many of the Old Testament writings of the prophets of old and the Psalms. Although, he knew the scriptures well and used them often to make a point, his teachings did not depend solely on these written words. While scribes waited for people to come to them to learn, Jesus went out to meet the people. The scribes taught in the synagogues; Jesus preferred the open air. No, Jesus was not a scribe.

Was Jesus a powerful guru? A guru is a preceptor who gives personal, religious or spiritual instruction, an advisor, a mentor, a teacher. Jesus performed most of these functions during his ministry, but he was not a guru. In the gospels, Jesus is referred to as "teacher" many times. Even his enemies considered him a teacher who taught "dangerous" beliefs. But, unlike the other teachers of his time, Jesus did not limit his teaching to men. He befriended women and included them in his most intimate circle of followers.

Some say Jesus was telepathic and clairvoyant, and that he possessed great psychic power. His actions among the people would make it appear that he was, yet, he attributed everything he did to the power of God. He told those who stood in awe of what he did that they could do as much and more if only they believed. Because of the healings he performed among the people, many wanted to make Jesus a political liberator.

Early in his ministry Jesus fought off the temptation of self-sufficiency, fanaticism in faith, and self-ambition. Yet, throughout his ministry there were those who would make him a rescuer king. One disappointed follower of Jesus lamented after Jesus died, "We had hoped that he was the one to redeem Israel." (Luke 24:21)

Even at the beginning of his ministry, Jesus let it be known that his mission among the people was prophesized in scripture. He read from the holy text in the synagogue: "The Spirit of the Lord is upon me, because he has anointed me to bring good news to the poor. He has sent me to proclaim release to the captives and recovery of sight to the blind, to let the oppressed go free, to proclaim the year of the Lord's favor." (Luke 4:18)

Jesus saw himself as the servant of those whom he loved, but he was also their foundation. "I am the good shepherd," he said to his followers. "The good shepherd lays down his life for the sheep." (John 10:11)

The words of Jesus were profound, yet simple. He knew that there were those in his midst who were too sophisticated to understand what he said. This saddened him because he could not reach them.

Much of what Jesus taught sounded like poetry. He used metaphors, paradoxes, and Galilean folklore. His words were vivid and exciting and he spoke with confidence and conviction. Some of the parables that he told were his, others were borrowed from the rabbis, but he offered them with a vigor and power that had not been heard before.

Jesus spoke in symbolic language. His ideas were sometimes put into visual form which made them crystal clear to those who would open their ears and hear. Other times, he would use riddles that could be understood by some and not by others. He used the vernacular to communicate; he taught with fiction to keep their attention; and he was not afraid to use sarcasm when necessary to make his point. He would take life situations and use them to teach a lesson.

As far as it is known, Jesus did not write down his teachings, but relied instead on the spoken word. Much of what he taught was passed on orally to others after his death.

When Jesus finished speaking to a crowd, Scripture says that "...the crowds were astounded at his teaching, for he taught them as one having authority, and not as the scribes." (Matthew 7:28)

Jesus knew the religious law well and did not oppose it; but he added to it in very original ways. "Do not think that I have come to abolish the law or the prophets; I have come not to abolish but to fulfill. (Matthew 5:17) When he referred to the sacred texts, he added his personal belief that even more was asked of those who professed to love God.

First, Jesus would cite the scripture. "You have heard that it was said to those of ancient times, 'You shall not murder;' and 'whoever murders shall be liable to judgment.' But I say to you that if you are angry with a brother or sister, you will be liable to judgment; and if you insult a brother or sister, you will be liable to the council; and if you say, "You fool," you will be liable to the hell of fire." (Matthew 5:21)

Jesus' personal belief in the immanent realm of God filled his teachings with immediacy and passion. His appeal was not legalistic, but filled with grace and beauty, truth and inspiration.

Jesus called on those who would listen to him to release the tremendous energies of the human spirit into the world. He grew impatient sometimes at the details of religious etiquette which the rabbis emphasized. He was focused not on the letter of the law, but the spirit of the law; and his ethics had to do with the individual responsibility of each man and woman as they came face to face with God in their daily lives.

Jesus did not call on people to abandon their religion, but to return to the heart of it. He admonished them not to be stuck in the rigidity of ritual and tradition, but to include justice, mercy, and faith in all they did.

It was not piety or self-righteousness that Jesus offered, but aliveness and vitality in living. Jesus appealed to conscience. He was not a rebel; he abided by the rules where he could; but when the rules were placed above basic human need, Jesus responded to the need regardless of the rule.

Jesus did not offer abstract philosophy or a universal religion. Instead, his ideas and his attitudes were presented as a practical way of life, and a transformation of existing religious practices. Jesus' foundation was Jewish and what he taught was based on what he had learned of life from his Jewish mother, and of the world from his Jewish father who mentored him in his carpentry shop.

The only thing the gospels reveal about the youth of Jesus was that he was deeply interested in religious matters. As a boy of twelve, his parents found him dialoguing with teachers in the temple.

Jesus was probably not formally educated. He was poor in his adulthood and without political influence or social standing. Yet, the intensity of his personality awed the powerful and confounded the wise.

Jesus was a dreamer, a poet, a lover of gardens and children. He brought the feminine energy that was within him into the midst of men toughened by the rigors of life. His was not an esoteric, big sky approach to life, but an absorption in a heavenly truth that permeated life in all its beauty and all its grotesqueness.

Jesus was a soul absorbed in God. He needed solitude. He fasted and prayed much of the time. He spent entire nights communing with God. He knew that the only way to be with and for others, the only way he could teach them as he did, was if he could enter into solitude to pray and be restored. His singleness-heartedness enabled him to be for others. He knew that, of himself, he had little to offer; connected to God, he could offer heaven itself.

Jesus taught his followers to pray. He considered prayer not as a duty to perform, but as a natural, spontaneous interaction with the Divine. For Jesus, all religion and all ethics could be reduced to the simplicity of two biblical commandments: To love God completely, and to love one's neighbor as oneself. His main theme in all he said to his followers was that God loved them unconditionally.

Jesus spoke of God in reverent terms, and yet, his words revealed a wonderfully close and intimate relationship with God. This unprecedented familiarity with God he offered to others as faith. For Jesus, the God of the masses was also the God of the individual. He taught that each person could have a personal, private, and intimate connection with God.

Jesus revered human nature. He had great hope in humanity and called forth the potential of each individual. Basically, Jesus believed that human life was sacred, and that God willed every human being to live life fully and authentically. He believed in the freedom of the human will, and never imposed his will on others. He invited men and women to change their lives and he left it up to them whether or not they would.

Holy Child

Star of the Desert

Ours is a pilgrim spirit, ever searching, ever moving toward the presence of God.

The journey of life is long and arduous, and the night is dark and cold. Yet, we trek across this wilderness for one small glimpse of God. But where are we to find God? Guide us, star of the desert; point us toward the place of God's abode.

We have been told to seek God in majestic temples, and in sacred books. They say to find God in the clouds above, and on the mountaintop. But we have searched in all those places and God is not there to be found. So, our search for God continues as we move across the land.

Guide us, star of the desert; tell us where God is. We are led to a place along the way where we see a woman, old and ragged, caring for those whose fortune is even less than hers. She looks at us and smiles as though she were a queen. We move along, still searching for our God.

Guide us, star of the desert; let us see God now. We are led to another place where we come upon a leper with open sores and bleeding stumps. We are repulsed at this grotesqueness, and we flee as fast as we can move, still searching for our God.

Guide us, star of the desert; reveal God to us. Then we are led to another town where we meet a merchant trading slaves, each one in chains, each one stripped of human dignity. One of them begs for a drink, but lest we offend the merchant, we move along, still searching for our God.

Guide us, star of the desert; bring us to God's presence. By the side of the road is a beggar man, kneeling down and looking up. He reaches out his hand in hope of holy alms, but there are so many like him, and we cannot respond to all; so, we just move along, searching for our God.

Guide us, star of the desert; let us be with God. And now we come to yet another town. We move through the mass of people crowding the streets, blocking our path. Don't they know that we are on a mission? How dare they slow us down!

As we make ready to leave this little dusty town, we come to a stable that shelters stock. There in the corner of the little sty, a man crouches in the cold of night, holding tight his pregnant wife, who appears close to her time. They are alone. He calls for help. But what can we do? We are not midwives; we dare not get involved. We must move along, searching for our God.

On entering the house, they saw the child with Mary,

his mother; and they knelt down and paid him homage.

Matthew 2:11

Shepherds and Astrologers

Regardless of who we are or what lifestyle we live, we cannot know God except in the still, silent night of the soul.

Some of us are shepherds – simple, hard-working, down-to-earth people. We mind our own business and, although we do not have a lot of book learning, we believe in God. Some of us are astrologers – learned, technical, dependent on others for information, seeking, keeping our eyes on the stars, looking for signs that will lead us to God.

As shepherds, we know about aloneness and are used to the silence of the hills. Not knowing, we live by faith. Yet, we are asked to come and see. We are asked to know God by leaving our posts and venturing into the valley where we can behold life and become a part of it.

As astrologers, we depend on our calculations. We measure our steps by what we know for sure, and act according to that information. Yet, we are asked to set aside our charts and figures. We are asked to disregard authority and signs. We are asked to trust our instincts, our emotions, and our spontaneity. We are asked to move toward God with nothing but our faith to guide us.

Whether shepherds or astrologers, we are called to know God through revelations we cannot anticipate. We may come seeking the spectacular, and discover simplicity. We may pursue the unusual, and encounter commonplace.

It is here, in the ordinary, that we come upon the Holy Child. He is heir to the kingdom of God and all its poverty. It is not what he will be that makes him eminent, but what he already is.

The Holy Child is poor; he has nothing save that which is given to him. He is powerless; he is at the mercy of others. He is weak and counts on the strength of others. He is vulnerable and may be taken advantage of. He is little, simple, and needy; he hungers and thirsts for nourishment and love.

It is before such a being that we discover the joy of life, which is complete dependence on God. We pay homage to the Holy Child and prostrate ourselves before him. We come to know God by looking upon the Holy Child, and experiencing the love that he brings forth from within each one of us. We will carry in our heart what we have beheld – the Holy Child, the hope of all the world.

Three Temptations

Into the Desert

Then Jesus was led into the desert by the Spirit to be tempted by the devil. He fasted forty days and forty nights, and afterward was famished. (Matthew 4:1,2)

We are called into the desert of the heart, there to become poor, hungry, and real.

It is in the dry and barren desert that we put away our desires for the superfluous and come face to face with our greatest need.

Our fast in the wilderness of life is not to be a display of asceticism, but a letting go of our self-sufficiency, and a fostering of our dependency on God. As we release our illusion of independence, we come to realize just how vulnerable we are.

The transition from the worldly to the spiritual is frightening to us because we hold so much. Temporal as they may be, we cling to self-sufficiency, religious fervor, and power because we think they are at least a foundation on which to count.

The wilderness through which we trek is a state of mind in which we find no landmarks to use as bearings. Everything seems to run together: good and evil, right and wrong, up and down, it looks the same to us.

We enter this arid region through a crisis, a deep conversion, or because life is changing too rapidly before our eyes. We long for the certainty of the law which tells us clearly and authoritatively what we must do. But in the desert, we are left alone, apparently without direction. Starved for purpose, thirsty for power, and lonely for the sense of self, we become prey to temptation.

The voice of temptation does not invite us to enter into evil; rather, it offers us something good, something in which we can believe. Otherwise, we would not be tempted. The subtle deception inherent in the tempting invitation is that we are promised more, but end up settling for less.

The temptations of self-sufficiency, fanaticism, and power lure us into dangerous territory by disguising themselves as our human need to be physically nourished, to believe in something greater than ourselves, and to have some control over our lives. We believe we are within reason and responsibility to pursue these prized possessions, so we approach the web of the spider that would entangle us in the silky chains of worldly desires.

We are driven into the desert with nothing to call our own except our soul. Left alone with our soul, the temptations disappear. Our soul has but one need – oneness with God. The temptation to surrender to the demands of our lesser needs fades quickly in the light of what is paramount to our soul.

First Temptation

The Tempter said to Jesus, "If you are the Son of God, command these stones to become loaves of bread." Jesus answered, "One does not live by bread alone, but by every word that comes from the mouth of God. (Matthew 4:3)

To acknowledge our need for earth-grown bread is to accept the nature of our humanity; to recognize our need for the word of God, is to embrace the essence of our divinity.

The temptation that Jesus encountered in the desert was the same temptation into which we all fall regularly. That is, to look upon God as a provider of our basic needs and our protector from harm. To focus only on this aspect of God is to misunderstand our relationship with the Divine.

Of course, we have basic needs that must be met if we are to stay alive. We must eat and drink and be sheltered and clothed. The satisfaction of these and other such needs is necessary for survival. Yet, the debate in the desert did not have to do with whether physical or spiritual food was more important. It had to do with the nature of God. The God in which Jesus believed is a God that gives us more than what we ask.

We ask God for the alleviation of pain. God offers us the ability to cope with pain, thereby loosening its grip on us.

We ask God to eliminate poverty in the world. God offers us the gift of compassion, which in turn motivates us to act on behalf of our fellow beings in creative and effective ways.

We ask God for peace in the world. God offers us peace in our hearts that we may spread peace in the world, beginning with ourselves, our family, and our immediate circle of influence.

We ask God for a piece of bread that we may be nourished physically and live for another day. God offers us manna from heaven, that is, love in our heart. There are children dying of malnutrition. Only the compassionate action that comes from love can alleviate their hunger.

Jesus believed in feeding the hungry, but not by invoking the direct power of God to do it. He believed that God works through us to feed, clothe, house, and otherwise care for the welfare of all human beings. God has already filled our hearts with compassion and our minds with creativity so that we may tend to those in our midst who are in need. The miracle that feeds the thousands is not based on power, but on the faith, hope, and love that God infuses into every living soul.

Second Temptation

The Tempter said to Jesus, "If you are the Son of God, throw yourself down; for it is written, 'He will command his angels concerning you,' and, 'On their hands they will bear you up, so that you will not dash your foot against a stone.'" Jesus said to him, "Again it is written, 'Do not put the Lord your God to the test. (Matthew 4:5)

God does not rescue us from our own folly.

The love God has for us allows us to enjoy or suffer the consequences of our actions and inactions. Some of us, however, confuse faith in God with fanaticism and act irresponsibly, believing that our reliance on God will exempt us from having to obey the laws of nature.

Some of us disregard the lessons nature has taught us and, instead, we ask for divine intervention to protect us. We tell ourselves that this is what Jesus meant when he said we could move mountains if we have enough faith. Is this what having faith is all about? Do we really have carte blanche with life if only we believe?

Does our strong faith in the power and goodness of God grant us dispensation from the law of cause and effect?

Our faith in faith can lift us off the ground and set us high above the rest of the world. Perched atop our misconception, we believe we can do anything we want with impunity. This is the temptation of fanaticism.

Jesus rejected the belief that if we are faithful, we will be immune from harm despite our actions. Faith in God must never contradict reason. Our faith must be framed in the reality of life. Faith includes rationality as well as emotion, logic as well as enthusiasm, and the mind as well as the heart.

During his ministry, Jesus' courageous acts of faith were not based on a belief in immunity, but on a belief that they were worth doing even when harmful consequences might ensue. Jesus did not choose the way of the Cross believing that he would be spared at the last moment. His faith was in the power of love, even through torture, even through death.

In life, we learn that even when we do our best to obey the laws of nature, harm may still come to us. It is then that our faith gets us through any ordeal. Our faith is not in a God who saves us, in spite of our rashness and stupidity, but in a God, who loves us so much that we are given the freedom, the responsibility, and the means to save or destroy ourselves.

Third Temptation

The Tempter offered Jesus all the kingdoms of the world and their splendor; and he said to him, "All these I will give you, if you will fall down and worship me." Jesus said to him, "Away with you, Satan! For it is written, 'Worship the Lord your God, and serve only him."" (Matthew 4:8)

The whole world and all its splendors fade away next to the bond we share with God.

For this reason, we were born; for this, we live; and for this, we die: that we may be one with God. The union between the Creator and the created, between the Lover and the beloved, between the Whole and the part, is our purpose in life.

Even so, we sometimes betray God. We may not actually scorn God, but we act in unfaithful ways. We may not disinherit ourselves from our Benefactor, but we flirt with attractive suitors. We may not deny our Source, but sometimes we wander away from it.

The temptation that lures us at every turn is not the temptation to choose shiny objects over God; rather, it is to not choose at all. The voice of temptation does not try to win us over. It distracts us and entices us to dislodge our focus on God. From this state of confusion and disintegration, we fall prey to the wolves that surround us.

When we lose our focus on God, we lower our consciousness and become easily lured away by the splendor of worldly treasures. We are offered the temporal kingdoms of power, possession, and pleasure; all we have to do is move our attention from God to something else.

To fall down and worship something means that we place ourselves at its disposal; that we declare our loyalty to it by our actions; that we become addicted to it by continually choosing it. It means that we deem it worthy of our respect, and that we, in fact, revere it.

For example, we may choose to become powerful in order that we may do good in the world. In our demanding pursuit of power, however, we lose contact with God, for whom we sought power in the first place.

Better to pursue our intimate relationship with God and let our love motivate our actions.

We may begin to accumulate material goods because they give us a sense of security. Soon, however, we find that possessions have a life all their own, and that they demand attention and protection. We learn very quickly that, "No one can serve two masters; for a slave will either hate one and love the other, or be devoted to the one and despise the other. You cannot serve God and wealth." (Matthew 6:24)

How then do we stay true to God? How do we keep our focus on God? How do we resist the temptation to leave? Each time, Jesus chose the higher power, the higher security, the higher joy. This was the secret of Jesus' faith: to stay focused on God at all costs; to love God so much that there would be little room in his heart for anything else. Jesus put God so high in priority, that he was able to reject tempting invitations to venture away.

This purity in heart, this singleness of purpose, this devotion to one love, was the essence of the gospel of Jesus; it was the meaning of his life and death; and it was how he transcended the crux of life.

Disciples

The Call of Discipleship

It took great discernment to choose the original twelve disciples.

Not everyone who wanted to be a disciple of Jesus was accepted to the group. Some were reluctant to leave everything and follow Jesus, but responded nevertheless to his compelling invitation.

Jesus called his disciples to something more than what they had known. To respond to his calling, meant leaving the comfort of the familiar, and losing themselves in something beyond themselves. It seems Jesus was the hardest, not on those who did wrong things, but on those who did nothing at all with their lives. As a leader, he asked his disciples for nothing less than everything. A disciple had to be ready to commit to Jesus; to leave all and not look back. "If any want to become my followers, let them deny themselves and take up their cross and follow me," Jesus said to his disciples. "For those who want to save their life will lose it, and those who lose their life for my sake will find it." (Matthew 16:24)

To be a disciple of Jesus when he was popular was not as hard as when he began to fall out of favor with the authorities. Then, it became dangerous to be with Jesus and many fled his side, though not the twelve.

Jesus experienced life with his disciples. He was with them at weddings, at funerals, at parties, and in the midst of storms. He was more than a teacher to them; he cared for them greatly and sought their welfare. One day, Jesus' disciples came back to him tired from a hard day's work. He said to them, "Come away to a deserted place all by yourselves and rest a while." (Mark 6:31) His compassionate words comforted even the most troubled and fatigued of his followers, "Come to me, all you that are weary and carrying heavy burdens, and I will give you rest. Take my yoke upon you, and learn from me; for I am gentle and humble in heart, and you will find rest for your souls. For my yoke is easy, and my burden is light. (Matthew 11:28)

Whatever else Jesus might have been to his disciples, he was their friend. He allowed a few to enter his intimate circle. He allowed himself to love them, and to enter into their joy and grief of life. "You are my friends...," he told them. (John 15:14) In his darkest hour, it was his disciples to whom he turned for support and consolation. They were all frightened and did not respond. One strayed and betrayed Jesus, yet Jesus still called him "friend."

Jesus knew that what he was teaching was hard to live by, and that those who dared to live according to his teachings would encounter much opposition and even torture and death. Toward the end of his life, Jesus tried to prepare his disciples for what they might encounter.

Even as Jesus faced the certainty of death at the hands of his persecutors, his focus was on those whom he loved. In respect and reverence, Jesus washed the feet of his disciples. In friendship, he ate his final meal with them. In devotion to their intimate bond, he prayed for them, "Holy Father, protect them in your name that you have given me, so that they may be one, as we are one...As you have sent me into the world, so I have sent them into the world." (John 17:11,18)

The Cost of Discipleship

The call to discipleship is alluring, but to respond to it we must be willing to pay the cost.

The call comes when we least expect it. We may be about our daily business; we may be in the midst of prayer; or we may be recreating ourselves in play and relaxation. We hear it, we see it, or we sense it; the call is clear and undeniable. We are asked to stop what we are doing and change the direction of our life.

Discipleship means "to follow." It means to learn the teachings of another, and to adhere to a way of life as lived out by the one we follow. To do this requires our willingness to surrender. But we have been conditioned to stay in control of all aspects of our life, and we are extremely reluctant to relinquish this control, even to God.

Now, we are asked to let go of our hold on what has been, and to allow the coming of what can be. To do this we must decide to risk leaving the secure known for the insecurity of the unknown. We must risk becoming vulnerable and afraid as we enter the uncharted waters of the soul. No longer are we to count on our self-sufficiency and strength; rather, we are to acknowledge our weakness and our dependence on something beyond ourselves.

In discipleship, we deny ourselves and follow our teacher. We do this not so much by depriving ourselves of what we want, but by focusing on what we truly need. Our teacher leads us in the paths toward the fulfillment of these basic needs.

As we respond to the call to discipleship, we abandon our attachment to the expectations of the world, and seek only the ways of peace and freedom. In our discipleship, we come to see ourselves as we are, nothing more and nothing less. From this level of humility, we dare to be ordinary and commonplace. We dare to be ourselves. We dare to love ourselves.

We carry out the mission of our discipleship, but we do so in the reality of who we are. We live and move and act according to our potentialities and our limitations. As disciples, we are not asked to withdraw from the world, but to enter into it fully, carrying with us the power of love.

"God is love, and those who abide in love abide in God, and God abides in them." (1 John 4:16)

Ministering Out of Their Resources

Jesus picked his twelve apostles and set about his ministry.

"He went on through the cities and villages, proclaiming and bringing the good news of the kingdom of God. The twelve were with him, as well as some women...who provided for them out of their resources." (Luke 8:1, 3)

The women who provided for Jesus and his apostles are mentioned only in passing, yet it was these women who facilitated the ministry of the men in the first place. They are also some of the disciples who later followed Jesus to Jerusalem and witnessed his crucifixion, death, burial, empty tomb, and resurrection appearances.

These women, who had evidently committed themselves to follow Jesus, were not preaching or proclaiming the good news, yet they were disciples nevertheless, doing their part "out of their resources." Perhaps they had wanted to preach to the crowds, but were denied the opportunity by Jewish customs. In any case, their contribution, which attracted little attention, was crucial in the overall ministry of Jesus.

A ministry can be one of high profile and of church-related activities. It can entail a special effort to serve a certain group; and it can even mean embracing a religious vocation. But ministry comes in many forms.

The common element among the various ministries is that those engaged in them are providing for others "out of their resources." This means using whatever talent or resource we have been given, and serving from whatever state in life we occupy at the moment.

Those whose ministries permeate everyday life in ordinary, inconspicuous ways, Jesus called "the salt of the earth," for it is their contribution that preserves and gives flavor to our lives. We all know people who are much like the women disciples of Jesus; people who daily offer to the world around them "out of their resources."

The doctor who does not belong to any organized social service organization, but who attends to patients diligently and with loving care is such a disciple.

The man who for 25 years has offered his customers a kind word and loving respect from behind his counter at the local post office is such a disciple.

The mother who nurtures her children, holds down a job to help support the family, and yet finds enough energy at the end of the day to sit and listen to a friend, is such a disciple.

The teacher who perseveres through the years, offering to young, formative minds the best that in him, is such a disciple.

The women disciples of Jesus, supported his ministry out of their resources, but remained unknown and unheraled. In like manner, the ministry we offer from our resources needs no credit, no publicity, no reward. All we need is to know that we are serving others in the name of God.

The temple of God is adorned by beautiful stained-glass windows and ornate altars from which the good news is proclaimed, but it is built of many small and inconspicuous bricks that serve as its foundation. In the same way, it is the hidden ministries that form the foundation of the kingdom of God.

Teachings

In the Heart of God

What could be more important than the power of God working through believers?

After all, isn't this the purpose of religion, to get all men and women to seek the will of God and do it? No. There is something even more important, something we tend to overlook.

Dozens of Jesus' disciples had been working faithfully among the people. They had been successful in healing the afflicted, and in freeing those who were bound by the chains of faithless living. The disciples came back from their mission excited to report to Jesus, "Lord, in your name even the demons submit to us!" (Luke 10:17) Their zeal was overwhelming. They had tasted the power of God working through their faith and dedication, and as far as they were concerned, they had completed their mission. Jesus said to them, "See, I have given you authority to tread on snakes and scorpions, and over all the power of the enemy; and nothing will hurt you. Nevertheless, do not rejoice at this, that the spirits submit to you, but rejoice that your names are written in heaven." (Luke 10:19)

Jesus was saying to his disciples, in essence, yes, God is powerful and, through you men and women of faith, God can do great and wonderful things. But the most wonderful thing of all, the greatest reason for rejoicing, is that each one of you is special to God. Each one of you is loved by God. Each one of you belongs to God.

It is one thing to be a soldier of God, and quite another to be the beloved of God. Jesus was saying to them that each disciple, in fact, each human being, has a place in the heart of God. No matter how we live or what we accomplish or don't accomplish in the name of God, each person is significant; each is cherished by God. After all, we can only love others because we have first been loved by God.

Jesus was saying that even spiritual power is not as important as the intimate and life-giving love of God. All else, including good works in the name of God, come from that. He was telling them to rejoice, not because with faith in God they could manipulate and control the world for good, but because they were loved by God. He was saying to them, rejoice, not because you have served God faithfully, but because God's love is yours even when you have not served faithfully.

Jesus was saying that those who believe that they will be loved by God only if they are good or only by serving others, are motivated by spiritual pride. He was telling them that the love of God cannot be earned or deserved. It is the nature of God to love.

Jesus loved to read the prophet Isaiah.

"Can a woman forget her nursing child, or show no compassion for the child of her womb? Even these may forget, yet I will not forget you. See, I have inscribed you on the palms of my hands…" (Isaiah 49:15)

Generosity

A crowd of thousands had gathered in the countryside to hear the words of Jesus.

The hour was late and the people were hungry. Because darkness would fall upon them before they could get home, they would stay there until morning. The disciples of Jesus were concerned for the men and women and their children. "Send the crowd away," they told Jesus, "so that they may go into the surrounding villages and countryside, to lodge and get provisions; for we are here in a deserted place." But Jesus said to them, "You give them something to eat." They said, "We have no more than five loaves and two fish – unless we are to go and buy food for all these people." (Luke 9:12, 13)

First, Jesus asked that the people get into smaller, more manageable groups and sit down in the grass. This way they could see each other's faces and perhaps get to know one another more as individuals than when they were just part of the mass.

Then Jesus took the scanty provisions that had been collected by the disciples; thanked God for them; and shared them with his disciples; who in turn shared from what they had been given. The people who observed Jesus and his disciples were inspired by their generosity and followed their example. Many in the crowd had brought no food with them, others had brought only a little. In smaller groups it was easier to determine who had food and who did not. Those who had food began to share with those who did not. The more that people shared with one another, the more onlookers were inspired to do the same. The spirit of generosity overcame the crowd. It was wonderful to feel; it was amazing to see; it was a miracle to experience.

We have all experienced this miracle when someone has shared with us from their limited means, only to inspire us to do the same with them and others less fortunate than ourselves. It is amazing how so little can do so much when it is shared.

The generosity that love inspires has to do with giving liberally from the heart. It does not mean that we share only from our surplus, but also from that which we cherish and need. We are not supposed to give it all away; rather, we are to love ourselves in the process and give to ourselves as well as others.

The spirit of generosity gives freely, without expectation of compensation or the acquisition of power, control, or credit. The spirit of generosity supersedes greed and insecurity. It is a spirit that is mindful that, in the final analysis, we are all one. After all, the word "generosity" derives from the word for *family.*

Forgiveness

Let anyone among you who is without sin be the first to throw a stone at her. (John 8:7)

With these words, Jesus answered the accusers of the woman caught in adultery.

He ignored their judgment and condemnation of her, and instead, asked them to focus on their own wrongdoing.

Standing before the crowd was a woman who had broken the law. She had not done so alone, but she was the one accused of the crime. Here was a group of men, armed with their code of law, and motivated by righteous indignation, calling for justice to be done. Here also, was Jesus who identified more with the lawbreaker than with the law enforcers. Jesus was looking, not at a mere criminal, but at a whole person. He knew that her broken life had not happened in a vacuum. With great compassion, he looked beyond her transgression to the needs of the total woman. He was not denying what she had been, but he believed in what she could be.

Instead of debating legalities with the self-proclaimed prosecutors, Jesus asked them to enter a higher court. He asked these men of the law to become men of the spirit. He asked them to look within themselves to see if they too had not done wrong. After all, we have all fallen down somewhere along the way. We have all made mistakes.

These men had heard Jesus say in the past, "Judge not that you not be judged." They had heard him pray, "...forgive us our debts as we also have forgiven our debtors." And he had already admonished them against living according to "an eye for an eye" mentality. Now he was saying much more. (Matthew 7:1, 6:12, 5:38)

He was asking them to go beyond mercy for the woman, and beyond forgiveness of her wrongdoing. He was asking them to identify with the adulteress, to be one with her, even in her brokenness.

If sin means turning our backs on God, then who of us is not a sinner? Of course, laws must be enforced for the protection of society as a whole, but the compassion and mercy that come with love need to be a part of our judicial process, and included in the way we treat those who have broken the law.

Identifying with those who violate the mores of society enables us to better understand them, and help them to make the return. By being one with them, we lend the force of our being to the reconciliation that can take place. Ostracism and punishment only alienate more and make more profound their woundedness.

When the men looked into their own hearts and identified with the woman, they realized that they were equally vulnerable to their weaknesses, and just as guilty in their own way. When they took on her imperfection, they had to leave, for they could not condemn her without also condemning themselves.

Left alone with Jesus, the woman felt no condemnation. Instead, she felt supported as a human being, in spite of her actions. She felt accepted as a sister, regardless of her reputation. She felt forgiven, even of her great indebtedness. She felt empowered to transform her life. Above all, she felt loved by the gentle man who could see into her soul.

No one had condemned her, including Jesus. Yet, when they were alone, he asked her to repent; to change her life, to break away from her lifestyle, to go her way and live with purity of heart.

Repentance

From that time Jesus began to proclaim, 'Repent, for the kingdom of heaven has come near. (Matthew 4:17)

Jesus' words could have been interpreted by his followers in two different ways.

Some might have understood them to be a warning. His words may have sounded like those of John the Baptist who seemed to be telling people to change their behavior before the impending fire and brimstone descended upon their heads. Some, on the other hand, knew that the word "repent" meant to see the error of one's way and to make a decision to change direction. They knew that it meant more than just saying, "I'm sorry. I'll be good from now on."

Repentance was to be taken seriously, according to Jesus, because it entailed reform. He taught that to repent meant that one had to re-prioritize one's life.

Jesus taught that it was not by willpower that his followers could change their lives. Rather, it was by accepting the reality that the kingdom of heaven was at hand, and by becoming a part of that kingdom.

The kingdom of heaven of which Jesus spoke was not a club that his followers could join, or a movement to which they could pledge allegiance. The kingdom of heaven, according to Jesus, was a power within all human beings, a power that only a few dared to evoke.

Jesus taught that, although one can will to behave decently; and will to follow the rules (civil or religious), that is all external. He believed that internal change, true repentance, happens only when one subjects himself or herself to the redeeming power of God's love.

Jesus was not admonishing his followers to hurry up and be good because the kingdom of heaven was gaining on them. He was announcing to them the good news that there was a power at hand, indeed within them, that could change them to be who they were meant to be.

As disciples of Jesus, we open our hearts to the kingdom of heaven and we notice the changes that come about. We find ourselves acting out of love instead of expediency. We dare to create instead of consume. We choose to spend time in prayer instead of oblivion. We stop to talk to a friend instead of rushing to accomplish a task. We reach for peace instead of grabbing for power. We give generously instead of hoarding selfishly. We respond to the needs of those around us instead of ignoring their plight. We courageously confront injustice instead of hiding our heads in the sand. We enjoy the fruits of life instead of losing ourselves in work. We use our God-given gifts with discipline instead of wasting our time and talent.

Because the kingdom of heaven is near, we evoke it, we repent, and we change our lives.

Teach Us to Pray

Jesus was praying in a certain place, and after he had finished, one of his disciples said to him, "Lord, teach us to pray...." (Luke 11:1)

Jesus said to his disciples, "Pray then in this way:

"Our Father in heaven, hallowed be your name. Your kingdom come, your will be done, on earth as it is in heaven. Give us this day our daily bread. And forgive us our debts, as we also have forgiven our debtors. And do not bring us to the time of trial, but rescue us from the evil one." (Matthew 6:9)

The power behind these words is in their reality to life. Jesus must have had this clearly in mind when he first said them to his disciples that day in the countryside. The words of Jesus' prayer speak about our relationship with God and with one another. They speak about our brotherhood, and they speak about love. They are words that can be internalized and lived.

Jesus' prayer is not so much a formula for living as it is a realization of who we are and what we are about.

Our ...

What a beautiful word, "Our" is. Only when two or more of us are considered together can we say "Our." It is a word that means community, family, joint ownership. What is it that we own together? What have we inherited? What do we possess already, even in our hearts?

...Father...

It is God who belongs to us and to whom we belong. We are held and loved and nurtured by Our Father. To recognize and to love God as Our Father, and each other as brothers and sisters was Jesus' message. This belief inspired his life and caused his death.

...in heaven...

Jesus taught that the kingdom of heaven is within us. It is into the sphere of our soul, then, that we must turn with singleness of purpose to find God. It is in the midst of ourselves that we discover that we are one with God.

...hallowed be your name...

We hallow (declare holy) God's name. We place God first and foremost in our life.

...Your kingdom come. Your will be done, on earth as it is in heaven...

The realm of God, the reign of love, is at hand; we need only believe it and subject ourselves to it moment by moment. Only by a faithful vigil can we ensure that God's will on earth (in our daily lives) will be done as it is in heaven (in our souls).

...Give us this day our daily bread...

We say "give" because what we receive is pure grace, it is not earned or deserved, but given with love. We subsist thanks to the daily food and drink that God's earth provides us; and we survive by the daily communion that God's kingdom of heaven offers us.

...And forgive us our debts, as we also have forgiven our debtors...

To live with the presence of God in our hearts is to let God live our lives. Only God's mercy moving through us, can forgive us and others for debts incurred.

...And do not bring us to the time of trial, but rescue us from the evil one...

Only love can keep us focused on God; only love gives us the devotion, courage, and perseverance to live for God alone.

Mary

Mary with Child

Yours is the womb that carries the Holy Child to fruition.

You allowed the Spirit of God to descend upon you, and have chosen to be the vessel of God's love. Be not afraid. Do not be troubled by this awesome responsibility. You need only be open to receive the Holy Offspring, and to remain one with him through the mystery of gestation. You are the servant of God. Let it be done unto you as it is willed in heaven.

There is nothing more intimate than the bond between a mother and her embryonic child. Their souls cannot be separated, even after birth.

Nurture the Holy Child; suckle him at your breast; invest yourself into his life. Offer him your sweet caress, your devoted attention, and your undying love. Cherish him with all your heart and soul. Let him know that he belongs, that he is wanted, and that nothing is more important to you than his well-being. Let him grow in grace and wisdom.

Yours is a monumental responsibility. It is a birthing that continues, and a motherhood that is forever.

The Holy Child will not always fit snugly into your arms. As he develops and moves out into the world, there will be times of pain and trouble. The time will come when the Holy Child will not fit into the world; he will be hated and scorned. One day, your heart will be pierced with the sword of grief. As he moves and acts according to the will of God, your Child will be rejected, persecuted, tortured, and killed. His rejection will be yours; his persecution will be yours; his torture will be yours; and his death will be yours. Mary, servant of God, in life and in death, the mother of the Holy Child you will always be.

Blessed Mary

Blessed is the womb that bore you and the breasts that nursed you. (Luke 11:27)

These are the words of a woman in the crowd who was moved by the teachings of Jesus.

Jesus looked at her and responded, "Blessed rather are those who hear the word of God and obey it!" (Luke 11:28) With these words, Jesus was making a significant statement about his mother. Certainly, Jesus would acknowledge that his mother Mary had conceived him, nurtured him within her womb, and labored painfully to bear him. He knew that it was at her breasts that he was nourished. But to Jesus, the motherhood of Mary meant much more.

Jesus believed that he was not only the fruit of her womb, he was also the fruit of all she was before and after his birth. Jesus knew that before Mary was his mother, she was a daughter of God. Jesus was saying, in his response to the woman in the crowd, that his mother was more than a vessel that carried him into the world; she was also a person alive, vital, and faithful. She was among those "…who hear the word of God and obey it."

Jesus gave his mother credit for giving him life, but her real gift to him had more to do with who she was and how she influenced him throughout his life.

Historically, we know little of Mary. We know her mainly through the son she raised. Theologians and church fathers have made Mary out to be the model for women. She was, according to the traditional image, passive, quiet, pious, untouched by passion, and willing to sacrifice. She was there, in the background, the silent sufferer.

This is the picture of the mother of Jesus that women have been asked to emulate and men have been led to idolize through the centuries. As it turns out, this "Madonna" image has been more of a curse for women, especially mothers, than it has been a blessing. This model has helped men to keep women in a secondary place, albeit an elevated place. Madonnas are placed on a pedestal and revered as special and holy. The only problem with treating women in this way is that they are stripped of their personhood.

Mary was a Jew living at a time when women were restricted by men from the privileges that men enjoyed. She was a faithful Jew and probably did not go against the accepted customs and traditions; but to make her out to be an acquiescent, static statue of a person, is to ignore her womanhood.

Jesus did not mature into who he was in a vacuum. His parents had much to do with who he was and what he believed. Jesus treated women with high respect as equals. This reflected how he felt about his mother. Jesus befriended women. He evidently did not subscribe to the notion that women were not to dialogue about spiritual matters. He trusted women, helped them, and accepted help from them without feeling his manhood was threatened.

The woman who influenced the life of Jesus probably more than any other person was his mother. She was alive and dynamic. She focused on God with all her love, and lived according to God's will. Her ways called Jesus out of himself and inspired him to be who he could be. Her communion with God impelled her to be open to possibilities and hopeful even in difficult times. From Mary, Jesus learned to be sensitive, receptive, creative, as well as strong, assertive, intellectual, and courageous.

Mary was a fountain of love and energy because she was, first and foremost, a contemplative. It was from Mary, who "pondered things in her heart," (Luke 2:19) that Jesus may have learned to pray and repose in the desert.

Jesus had studied the laws and the prophets which Mary probably had not. He learned right from wrong from the way his mother lived; and he gained a sense of justice from his father Joseph, who was a "just man," (Matthew 1:19).

Jesus' love of nature must have been promoted by someone who also loved nature. Can you picture Mary showing little Jesus the wonder of a bug, the growth of a flower, and the flight of a butterfly? Mary's down-to-earth approach to life must have influenced Jesus if we judge by the parables he told. Mary knew how to love unconditionally and this, above all, was her legacy to

Jesus. Before he could preach about the power of love, he had to have experienced it in his own life.

All we have to do is look at Jesus to discover the full womanhood of Mary. Blessed was the fruit of her womb; but not just because she cherished him, and treated him lovingly. Jesus was who he was in part because Mary probably challenged him, differed with him, and confronted him from time to time. Against the walls of her confrontation, Jesus strengthened his wings before he ventured out into the world.

Let us see the Mary who gave birth to a son and held him closely to her bosom, wanting never to separate from him. But let us also see the Mary who had the courage to let him go, first in life and then in death.

The faith of Mary included not only her willingness to listen to the word of God, but also to respond to it with her life. Mary, the integrated woman, must have experienced some dark nights of the spirit, during which she did not understand, and yet believed and waited for her time.

Mary was full of grace, not because God favored her above others, but because she was conscious of God's unconditional love for her and for her son. Mary was immaculate, not because she was spared the agony and the ecstasy of being human, which she was not; but because she evoked the force of God from within herself. She embraced her integrity as a woman; and she lived her life as a daughter of God.

The Beloved of Jesus

Joseph

Joseph was a quiet man.

Joseph was not one to bring attention to himself or to put on airs despite his royal lineage. In fact, the Scriptures hardly mention him. We know he was a good and righteous man, just and tolerant, wise and faithful. He seemed content to be a part of the foundation from which his son Jesus would launch his ministry.

Surely, Joseph influenced Jesus in his youth. He taught him a craft with which he could make a living. He taught him about the practical things of life, and he taught him about simplicity and honesty. From Joseph, Jesus learned about loyalty and devotion, and about the sanctity of family. As a devout Jew, Joseph passed on to Jesus his religious traditions, and more, he exemplified a strong love of God and a desire to obey God's will.

Above all, Joseph was there, dependable, reliable, secure, and available. It was with this as a background that Jesus began his life.

Perhaps you know a Joseph in your life. Maybe you are a Joseph. Josephs are very special people. They are the ones who make things happen; they provide the shoulders on which others can stand to reach the stars. A Joseph doesn't get much credit. Usually, he or she is in the background, unnoticed, yet, vital to any operation. Without a Joseph in their lives, I wonder how far the great men and women of history would have gotten.

A Joseph personality is usually down-to-earth, somewhat analytical, practical, and matter-of-fact about things. Often, a Joseph is good at technical skills, and the handling of facts and objects. Besides quiet, a Joseph can be serious. He or she is able to concentrate on the task at hand and to be thorough in what is done.

A Joseph is practical, orderly, and logical. Dreamers sometimes have difficulty with this type of person because a Joseph is so realistic about everything. Organization is a strong suit of a Joseph, as are responsibility and determination. A Joseph is tenacious if he or she believes strongly in something or someone.

The artists, the politicians, the entertainers, and all the great male and female heroes of the world have probably had a Joseph in their lives, someone on whom they could rely for the basic support they needed so desperately. A Joseph brings framework to possibilities, order to chaos, and implementation to plans. A Joseph complements the more philosophical personality by anchoring it in reality.

In our world, we don't pay much attention to the Josephs. We take them for granted. Our focus is more on those who offer inspirational dreams, the dreams that are later realized by Josephs. Where the charismatic leader is apt to get bored and move on to something else, the Joseph dares to stay until the job is finished. Without the Josephs in the world, all the imaginative ideas would blow away with the wind.

On a holy night long ago, a young, frightened woman gave birth to the baby who was to lead men and women back to God. It was Joseph who was there to comfort the mother. It was Joseph who was there to midwife the most important event ever. And it was Joseph who was the first to hold the Holy Child and to give him his first taste of human love.

Martha and Mary

Martha, Martha, you are worried and distracted by many things; there is need of only one thing. Mary has chosen the better part, which will not be taken away from her. (Luke 10:41)

Oh Lord, how you loved us!

We were your friends and followers; yet, we were more like family. The best day of my life was the day you came to our village of Bethany to teach our people, and I welcomed you into our home.

You befriended me and my sister Mary, and later, my brother Lazarus. Our friendship was long-lasting and life-giving. Your presence in our home was always so uplifting. We talked, we laughed, and we shared our meals together.

I think you enjoyed coming here to rest. Your ministry was so demanding, and this was a place where you could come for some repose. You cared for so many, and here, we could care for you.

Mary loved you. She snuck into Simon the leper's house when you were dining there with others, to pour ointment on your head. You forgave her all her sins. You changed her life. Lazarus loved you. When he became ill and died, you wept for him and for his family; then, you came to call him back to life. I too, have loved you.

Mary showed her love for you by giving you her single-hearted attention. I have shown my love for you by tending to your human needs: nourishment, shelter, unconditional acceptance, and a sense of belonging. Each in our own way, Mary and I have tended to your needs. This has been our purpose: to be the salve that soothes your soul along the way.

Peter

You called me Peter.

You called me "the rock," yet, I was but a pebble, tossed and turned in a river of emotion. I was frightened, I was excited, I was impulsive and compulsive. I was ready to offer you everything one moment, and to take it back the next. I was a believer full of doubt; a follower who fell behind. I was willing, but I did not understand.

When you came to me, I was surprised. Why would I be taken into the inner circle of the Teacher? Why would I be chosen from among the crowd? I was impure and I was worldly. I was a simple fisherman. What business did you have with me? When you called me to follow you, I did not hesitate. I dropped my nets, I left my boat, I said goodbye to those I loved. I was inspired by your words, although I did not understand them.

You called me "the rock," yet, I faltered many times. I was tested in the water as I moved toward you, but then I looked away. I was frightened by the wind; I lost my focus and I began to sink. Even then, you caught me and rebuked me for my lack of faith.

It was I who first received the insight that you were one with God. You blessed me, and you called me the foundation of your church. You entrusted me the keys of the kingdom and the power to bind and to set free. It was also I who soon thereafter tried to hold you back from your mission. I wanted to protect you from the dangers that I saw. You rejected my control. I did not understand.

Again, you trusted me. You took me high upon a mountain, there to be with you. It was strange the way you prayed, the way you changed, the visions that I saw that day. You had let me witness the communion of souls. You had given me a glimpse of the eternal. Yet, even as I stood among the spiritual, I depended on the material. I wanted to build something solid to memorialize what could not be explained. I wanted to capture the ephemeral. In my enthusiasm, I had missed the point again. You told me to say nothing, and do nothing, just to let it be. I did not understand.

When you told us you must leave us, I wanted to go with you. I vowed my allegiance and proclaimed that I would follow you into prison and into death itself. You predicted I would deny you even before the dawn.

After you nourished us with food, you stopped to wash our feet. I objected. It was below your status, I said. Afterall, you were a king, not a servant, I argued. I would have none of it. Once again you rebuked me. Either I be made clean by you or I would have no more to do with you. My feet were washed, and I was humbled by your grace.

I told you time and again that I would be with you forever. But when you asked me to stay with you one hour in the garden to pray and watch, I fell asleep. You were full of dread and sadness, yet I let you down when most you needed me.

When they came for you, I felt so helpless. I, who had echoed your call for peaceful ways, took a sword and struck at the enemy. Again, you rebuked me, reminding me of the nature of your mission.

Without a sword in my hand, I was frightened. I withdrew into the shadows. I followed at a distance as they took you away into the darkness.

Then I was confronted. Was I with you? No, I said. Did I know you? No, I said. Did I follow you? No, I said. Just then, you turned and looked at me. Your loving eyes pierced my heart and I ran away in bitter tears. I had abandoned you again.

I did not have the courage to go to Golgotha. I would be crucified. I stayed away until I heard that you had died.

Though I had not understood, though I had weakened and abandoned you; you saw something in me that I did not see in myself. From the beginning, you must have known that, in the end, it would be I who would gather your scattered flock; it would be I who would be lifted by grace alone. It would be I who would follow you. even unto death.

Even in spirit, you came to me again. You offered me nourishment. Once again, you asked for my assent.

Three times I had denied you; three times you asked me if I loved you; three times I answered yes. Three times you asked me to tend to your sheep; to care for those you loved. You trusted me to be the bearer of your message. I faltered, I doubted, I hesitated. Then I remembered your words. "And I tell you, you are Peter, and on this rock, I will build my church, and the gates of Hell will not prevail against it." (Matthew 16:18)

John

I was among the first to follow you and the last to leave your side.

You called me your disciple; you called me "Son of Thunder," and you called me your beloved friend. I was your disciple in many ways. You were the eloquent teacher and I was your eager student. You were the master and I was the novice. You were my elder brother and I, the youngest of the disciples, looked to you as the model for my fledgling manhood. I learned so much from you about life, about love, about God, and about myself.

I followed you as you trekked the dusty roads; and I followed you into the towns. I followed you to the mountaintop; and I followed you into the garden. I was with you when you played with children and laughed with friends. I was with you when you spoke to the multitudes and when you spoke to God. I was with you when they cheered you; and I was with you when they jeered.

You took me from the shores of Capernaum and led me to new life; but on the way I pushed and pulled to satisfy my will. I was a "Son of Thunder" as you had well observed. I bolted and I scandalized, and I made a lot of noise. I thought I knew what we were doing, but I did not really understand.

Where I had been prideful, you taught me humility. Where I had been vengeful, you led me to mercy. Where I had been critical, you showed me forbearance. I wanted to be the greatest, you asked me to be the least. I wanted to be first, you asked me to be last. In my spiritual ambition, I wanted to be seated at your right hand in the world to come. Instead, I was placed at the foot of your cross in the world I was in.

I was your beloved friend. You trusted me; you kept me close; you included me in your personal life. There was a bond between us that could not be explained. You loved the others as much as me, yet, there was something else. We were connected at the level of the soul.

Through the time we had together, you allowed me the intimacy of close companionship, and let me know your mystical self. Engrossed in the powerful words you uttered, and secure in the gentleness of your spirit, I stayed. I watched as you entered into prayer. It was not ritual; it was not rote. For you, it was an entry into the heart of God. Perhaps this was our special link: that we shared the reality of your transcendental self, the freedom of your boundless nature.

Then they tore you from our midst; and they nailed you to a cross. It was my flesh they were piercing, my body they racked. I was afraid like all the others, yet, I could not leave you then. You needed me there, if only as a friendly face. I felt so helpless, so useless, so weak. There was nothing I could do. I would have died for you, yet, I was forced to live and watch you die instead.

From the pit of your despair and the agony of your crucifixion, you turned to me once more. You entrusted me your grieving mother, who now would be alone. You believed that I could carry on the work that you had started; and you relied on me to tend to the one who once had tended you.

When you died, I died; now you live on in me.

Judas

I have betrayed you, Jesus, and I have betrayed myself.

From the beginning, I did not understand you. You seemed so out of touch. I was about causes and politics; you were about love and God. I was focused on externals; you looked within. I was governed by the opinion of others; you were willing to move against the wind.

I did not understand you, Jesus. It seemed so right to me that we should use the clout of your popularity to bring good things about. You could have been king, if only for a little while. You seemed so esoteric. We needed to feed the hungry and clothe the naked, yet, you were advocating forgiveness of the oppressors. We needed force to gain the upper hand; but you spoke of peace through meekness. We needed to organize our strength; you asked us to acknowledge our weakness. We needed to fight back, to rebel; you only turned the other cheek.

We needed to count on ourselves; you wanted us to depend on God.

I did not understand you, Jesus. You dreamed of a kingdom that I could not see. You believed in a force that I could not feel. You counted too much on faith, and not enough on reality. You seemed to always be in prayer, even when the forces of evil ran rampant through our land. Despite my warnings, you would not veer from your collision course. I would not be a part of your insanity.

I did not understand you, Jesus. I, who was among your followers, had not trusted you. I began to doubt. I began to fear the consequences of following your path. I chose, instead, my own approach. Moved by my own illusion, I turned my back on you. I placed my faith in the hierarchy of the world. I looked to them to put things right. I did not realize that they feared you greatly. I did not realize that they would use my zeal against the higher good. I did not know I was sending you to be slaughtered at the hands of pseudo power.

I, who had been entrusted with the purse of our community, turned to those who called you "enemy." I brought them to your private place. I told them where you were. With swords and clubs, and the force of men, we came upon you in the night.

Even as I approached you, my mind became confused. I had believed so strongly that I was right. Now I did not know for sure. I loved you so; yet, I wanted something else. I called you Master; though I followed you no more. I kissed you; but I no longer felt you close.

Something was terribly wrong. I hoped you would flee and hide; yet, I knew you would not do that. I did not want to face you; yet, you looked into my eyes and called me "Friend." What had I done! What travesty! What error! Yet, it was too late.

As they led you from the garden, my heart exploded. I was slipping from your grasp. I was sinking into the mire of my deed. I could not bear the pain.

I did not understand you, Jesus. You were more than I could comprehend. I did not understand that the power of your love transcended the power of all else. I did not understand that when you called me "Friend" you had forgiven me.

I walked toward my tree of death, still believing in my own power to end the pain. "I have sinned by betraying innocent blood." (Matthew 27:4) I returned the silver, but it was not about the silver. I repented what I had done; but I could not now undo it. I had dammed myself to perdition; I had led to slaughter a lamb of God. Blinded by the tears of my remorse, I did not see that even from the Cross, you still were loving me.

Mary Magdalene

I came to you confused and broken, Rabbi; you took my hands and looked into my eyes; quietly, you talked with me; gently, you restored my soul.

I was the victim of my unloved self. I was caught in the snares of perdition, living at the surface of my being, for I dared not look within. Mine was a dreadful existence with no purpose but to move from day to day with some semblance of life.

One day I heard your voice. It soothed me and it troubled me. The words you spoke to the crowd were gentle, but direct; and you spoke as if to reach my heart. You did not judge nor did you shame; you offered healing, even to my darkened soul.

With you, I felt significant. I was only one of many in the crowd; yet, I felt personally and unconditionally accepted by you. It was as if I had always known you, and as if I would always know you. The hardness of my heart softened, and the flower of love began to blossom.

Now I felt the stirring of my private self. Now I felt emotions once again. I felt guilt, I felt repentance, I felt hope, and I felt alive. I heard you say that it did not matter as much where I had been as where I was going. You offered me forgiveness, and you offered me your love.

Yours was not a common love. It was more than I could bear. It touched me deep within, and it changed what I had been. No longer would I be a victim of my circumstance, but a woman prepared to overcome adversity, willing to learn and obey the will of God. I, sensed within me my virgin soul.

I did not understand you; yet, you made much sense. I did not believe you; yet, my heart was full of faith. You were not like other men whom I had known. You had the firmness of a man and the tenderness of a woman. You emanated strength; yet, allowed your vulnerability. You were just a wanderer; but your words had the roots of a cypress tree and the permanence of heaven. I cried from the sadness of the life I had led, and I cried from joy of the life that now was mine.

The ecstasy of my salvation gave way to the agony of Calvary. Why would they do this to such a man? Why would they destroy this fountain of love?

They kept me at a distance, but I could not stay away. I broke through and ran to the foot of your Cross. There, I fell to my knees in disbelief and painful sorrow. How excruciating! How helpless! I would stay there to the end.

I had known the joy of life and now my life was over. Your life awakened the spirit within me, and your death had drowned me in its wake. My only purpose now was to anoint your lifeless body before they buried you. But even this last gesture of my love was taken from me because they took you away to be buried.

I was there when they laid you in a tomb and rolled a stone to close the opening. After the Sabbath, I returned to the tomb. As I approached the place where they had laid you, I discovered that the tomb was open, and your body was not there. I was filled with amazement and terror at the same time. I wept from the core of my being.

"Woman, why are you weeping?" asked a stranger in the garden. You were that stranger, but I did not recognize you until you said my name. "Mary," you called, as you had so many times before. "Rabbi," I answered, for I knew you had returned. I could not touch you as before; you were not there to stay. Yet, I knew that in my heart, you would always be.

Beatitudes

Jesus spoke from his heart as he revealed the secrets of life.

Not wealth, but poverty turns us to God, he said. And only when we are open to the pain of life, are we also open to the comfort that comes from God. The young teacher talked of meekness, littleness, and humility as a way to stay grounded in the reality of who we are and who God is in us. He said that only a yearning for the ways of God would keep us ready to receive, and he talked of letting go of that which blocks the flow of love.

Jesus said that through the forgiveness of ourselves and others we are made whole again, and that our focus on God, even through the dark moments of our life, enables us to experience the presence of God. Jesus spoke of peacemaking as an integral part of our human mission, and an inherent part of our divine nature; and he spoke of the essential willingness to face even the worst consequences of doing the will of God.

The powerful words of Jesus offer us more than principles of goodness and piety; they guide us to our full potential as human beings and offspring of God. They are a way of life. His words do not tell us what to do, but what to be. They lead us toward the highest realization of ourselves.

Blessedness is more than happiness; it is a joy in the soul that no outward circumstances can seriously affect. Blessedness is connectedness with God; it is the enjoyment of intimacy with the Divine. Blessed are we who listen to the words of Jesus and live by them, for we shall be in harmony with heaven.

Poverty

Blessed are the poor in spirit, for theirs
is the kingdom of heaven. (Matthew 5:3)

At the core of our soul, we embrace the nature of our humanity, which is poverty.

But embracing our poverty does not mean that we become passive victims of life. It means that we recognize our weakness, and invoke the strength of God; we admit our fear, and receive the courage of God; we declare ourselves lost, and take the guiding hand of God; and we deem ourselves poor, and are enriched by the gift of God's love. It is only when we surrender to our powerlessness, and acknowledge our utter dependence on God that we can be helped.

Poverty of spirit is not an option; it is our reality. It is not a virtue for which to strive; it is our nature. It has to do with our attitude toward what we have or don't have. To be poor in spirit is not a matter of suppressing our personality, and it has nothing to do with asceticism. It has to do with remaining true to our humanity, because to be human is to be poor, and, in the final analysis, we are all beggars.

As we accept our poverty, we release our illusion of security, power, wealth, and any other treasure to which we cling. After all, the only real security is that which we receive from God's presence. It is not security from harm, but security that ensures the intactness of our soul. The only real power is that which emanates from God; everything else is relatively powerless. The only real wealth is that which we can store in the stronghold of our soul.

The divine paradox is that, when we let go of everything, we have everything. The kingdom of heaven is the source of life and love that we see in the life of Jesus, and which we too can have. It is freedom from the illusion of self-sufficiency; it is complete reliance on the God within. To live in the kingdom of heaven, is to exist in a different state of mind, a different level of consciousness. In our poverty of spirit, we lack everything except an intense longing to be touched by God. In our emptiness, we become a receptacle for the love of God. In our woundedness, we are bonded in compassion with a suffering world. In our incompleteness, we keep turning back to God. Darkness becomes our friend. In our weakness, is our strength. In our brokenness, we seek a wholeness that transcends the self. The other side of love is poverty. It is love that has impoverished us; and it is love that transforms our poverty into an abundant life in God.

Embrace your poverty. Your emptiness will be filled. Your brokenness will be mended. Set aside the illusion of your self-sufficiency. With your surrender comes the prevalence of God.

Grief

Our grief, if we allow it, becomes for us an act of love.

We have loved in life and our grief is a part of that love. It does not make sense for us not to grieve when we have loved and lost. We are wounded and in need of healing, and grief is a natural emotion; it is the course that leads us back to life.

Loss shakes our very foundation, and we are moved to a deeper part of our being. Our grief forces us to a depth of feeling that is below anything that we have consciously experienced before. We begin to feel the fears and insecurities of our past which we may have suppressed for some time. We are forced to endure a pain that we have not known. We hurt so much that we want to die; yet, it is a paradox because, as we enter into the pain of loss, we become more alive than we have ever been.

We are changed dramatically by our grief. We will eventually be all right, but we will never be the same. Our priorities are different after a loss. The things we held as so important become unimportant, and the things we thought were insignificant become paramount.

In the midst of our grief, it is very hard to pray. We become spiritually dry and it seems we've lost our faith forever. We feel abandoned by God in the midst of our travail. Eventually, we realize that God has been with us all the while, sharing our loss, our pain, our tears. God has been there all along, giving us the strength and courage to make it through the long and agonizing night.

Mourn your losses. Allow the pain of your loss to consume you. You will be given the courage to enter the dark night of bereavement. You will receive the strength to endure until the dawn.

Meekness

Blessed are the Meek, for they will

inherit the earth. (Matthew 5:5)

In our meekness, we are grounded in the reality of life just as it is.

In meekness, we declare ourselves open, available, and receptive to God. We are one with the whole world; and we are one with God. We enter into self-forgetfullness; and we go beyond ourselves to God.

We know that by ourselves we can do nothing. We move by the power of God; and when we realize this, and live accordingly, nothing is impossible to us. God works through us, when we allow it. But it takes courage to be meek because when we allow ourselves to be meek, we are left vulnerable before the world.

Meekness brings gentleness into our lives in the way we treat ourselves and others. Gentleness has to do, not so much with softness, as with consideration, thoughtfulness, and tolerance. Being gentle with others means that we are willing to provide a place for them in our circle of life. It means that we are able to become intimate with them, and have them feel welcomed by us.

In meekness, we are willing to "turn the other cheek;" but this does not mean that we invite harm to come to us. The spirit with us would have us defend and protect ourselves against harm of any kind. Turning the other cheek means that when we have been hurt by life, we are willing to live and love again, even at the risk of being hurt again.

Meekness includes humility, and in humility, we are willing to share our burdens with God; and we are willing to ask for help from one another. In humility we become grounded in the reality around us; and we are willing to be honest with ourselves and others. In humility, we acknowledge our weaknesses as well as our strengths. We realize our limitations as well as our potentialities. We let go of our inordinate ambition to be more than we are. We make the best of the conditions in which we find ourselves; and we develop all that has been given to us, and use it to the best of our ability. In meekness, we come to learn just how little control we have in life. We let go of our illusion of control so that God can take control of our lives.

Meekness signified for Jesus a dependence on a power greater than his own. There was a genuine humility about this man, who was acutely conscious of his own insufficiency apart from God.

The Hebrew derivation of the word "meek" connotes a disposition of the heart susceptible of being molded by the spirit of God. This seems to be the meaning Jesus gave to the word.

In your meekness, you are down-to-earth. In your humility, you accept yourself as you are. In your honesty, you acknowledge your potentialities, as well as your limitations. Your decision to drop away the masks you wear brings you the freedom to be real.

Yearning for the Ways of God

Blessed are those who hunger and thirst for righteousness, for they will be filled. (Matthew 5:6)

We belong to God, and nothing short of God can fulfill us.

Inherent in our being is a deep yearning to be one with God, and to be enveloped and sustained by the energy of God's unconditional love.

Righteousness goes beyond goodness and morality; it is the nature of God within us. It is how God lives and loves through us. Our tremendous appetite for God is intrinsic to our human nature; yet, how easily we go hungering and thirsting for that which cannot fulfill us. How often we pursue the treasures of our lesser selves. How sad when our desire for the things which do not last dulls our sense of appetite for that which is eternal.

Sometimes we mistake our hunger and thirst for God with something else. We choose whatever may assuage the pain of our hunger and thirst. But when we acknowledge and respond to our innate appetite for God and for God's order, all other appetites fade away in contrast.

Our soul is the place where we surrender all to our Beloved. It is here, that our body, mind, and heart are gathered. It is here, that God shows us a way to love that we have never known before. We cannot love God too much; we cannot desire God too intensely. This pull, this attraction, this hunger and thirst, is, in essence, God's passionate love for us being reflected back to God.

Yearn for and receive sustenance for your soul; thirst for and be given the nectar of God. Your desire for the will of God releases you from the snare of other appetites. You are filled with the Spirit of God.

Mercy

Blessed are the merciful, for they
will receive mercy. (Matthew 5:7)

Like the dawning of a new day, mercy grants a second chance at life.

Burdened by the weight of guilt, shame, and condemnation, we fall to our knees, there to plead for what we do not deserve and cannot earn. We beg forgiveness. God bestows mercy on us; takes our hand and lifts us up that we may walk.

No matter what we have done or failed to do, in the wake of our repentance, comes our absolution. We are forgiven, we are made whole again. God looks beyond our misdeeds to the state of our being, and believes in us even when we have stopped believing in ourselves.

We need to seek mercy from God; we need to seek it from those whom we have hurt; and we need to seek it from ourselves. Until we are willing to forgive ourselves, we are not open to forgiveness from God or others. Even as we pray for mercy, we do not pray for ourselves alone. Our prayer transcends the personal to include all who stumble along the path of life. We cannot separate ourselves from the transgressions of our brothers and sisters, for we are one with them even in sin.

We are changed by the mercy that is shown to us. Our self-righteousness turns into generosity; our indignation turns to compassion; and our sense of justice turns to mercy. Having been forgiven by God and by those whom we have hurt, we are moved to forgive those who have trespassed against us.

We restore the soul of those whom we forgive; we give new life where all seems lost; we heal the affliction that comes with guilt, and we pass on no less than we receive from the loving grace of God.

We are not compelled to befriend or even to like those whom we forgive. We are not asked to exonerate or justify the bad that others do, only to identify with their imperfection, and to grant them the mercy that we would ask for ourselves. Our forgiveness of others releases them from the bondage of their debt, and we, who forgive from the heart, are also freed from the chains of rancor and resentment.

Forgiveness does not happen in a single act, but is a process through which we gradually release that which we hold against another. The process begins when we first decide to forgive, and it concludes when we bring closure to the past and begin investing in the present.

Forgiveness is not a transaction in which we exchange mercy for mercy. God is the prime mover, the merciful one. What we receive from God, we give to ourselves and others; then, in God's mercy, we are transformed. In gratitude, we come nearer to God; in love, we dedicate ourselves to God; in faith, we surrender our life to the will of God.

Be merciful with yourself and others. You block love when you hold rancor or resentment in your heart. Do not wait for others to deserve or earn your forgiveness. Let it be your gift, without expectations.

Single-heartedness

Blessed are the pure in heart,

for they will see God. (Matthew 5:8)

To seek God with our whole being is the instinct of our soul.

For this we were born, to remain with God each day, in love and devotion; and to commune with God through the darkness and the unknowing. The heart is our core, our inner self, the seat of our mind and will. It is our source of life and the fountain of our love.

Purity in heart is a gift that God gives to us when it is clear that we want it. All we have to do is really want it.

In prayer, we become receptive to God's grace; in prayer, we make ourselves available for God's presence; in prayer, we open up our heart that God may love through us. God is with us every moment of our life.

Purity in heart is our awareness of that presence; it is our intense desire to be with God. From God we receive our self-identity, our love force, our purpose in life. God draws us and we respond.

God waits for our return and we long to go home. When we separate ourselves from God, we separate ourselves from ourselves. A heart divided cannot withstand the rigors of life. It seems the closer we get to God, the more painful our separation.

In purity in heart, that is, focus on God, we begin to see the good and the salvageable in all there is and in all that happens, even the vicissitudes of life. With God in our heart, ugliness can be beautiful, and misery can be joyful. When all else is less important than God, we come to see God in all things and in all persons. When God is paramount in our heart, the Divine is manifested in all occasions.

Seek God with your whole being; Your humanity instinctively reaches out to your divinity. Your heart cannot thrive disconnected from your Beloved.

Peace

Blessed are the peacemakers, for they will
be called children of God. (Matthew 5:9)

Peace is the consequence of letting go in faith, and waiting for God in trusting surrender.

Peace comes when we love God more than peace itself. God summons us into oneness, and it is this union with God that calms our rebelliousness. Try as we may, we cannot bring about peace by willing it or working for it. In fact, our inordinate desire for peace steals away our peace.

The healing peace of God is ours even in the midst of the tempest. We need not wait for the turmoil in our life to be calmed. Peace is more than calmness, tranquility, and harmony. It is believing in the integrative love of God, and resting in God's oneness, even as we are pulled in many directions. Peace can come to us at the worst times of our life, and regardless of the circumstances in which we find ourselves. It is not contingent on what is happening around us, but on what is happening within.

Peace can come in the midst of our suffering, even when we have been broken and scattered. It does not come because we remove our external problems, but because we become aware that we are not alone, even as we face those problems, whatever their magnitude. Peace comes, not as a result of our holding on to our will and control, but as a result of letting them go. We do not hold peace; we are held by peace.

Peace is the acceptance of the truth about ourselves; it is the embracing of our whole being, without judgment, condemnation, or denial. Peace comes to us when we allow ourselves to be who we really are. Facing the truth about ourselves and living in accordance with that truth, brings us into harmony with God and into congruence with the will of God.

Peace is not something we impose on others; instead, it is something we are to others. Having embraced the differences within us, we are more willing to allow and appreciate the differences in others.

We are peacemakers, but this does not mean that we turn away from confrontations which are sometimes necessary. To be at peace, we must be true to ourselves and sometimes this means that we must assert ourselves, and face the consequences. Internal peace sometimes means that we must be willing to live without external peace. The way of peace is not always the path of least resistance.

When we are at peace with ourselves and with God, we are at peace with others. Peace is with us because God is with us. The God of peace that abides within each one of us is the hope for all humanity.

Peace be with you. Let it be a peace that brings rest to your weary body, a peace that soothes your troubled heart, a peace that brings light even in darkness, and joy, even in the midst of sorrow.

Persecution

Blessed are those who are persecuted for righteousness'
sake, for theirs is the kingdom of heaven. (Matthew 5:10)

Living in accord with the divine principle is our prime
responsibility in life.

Righteousness means the way of God. Sometimes,
however, our fidelity to God and to God's way can place
us at odds with the world around us. To be persecuted
means to be made to suffer because of something we
believe. We believe in the way of God.

With courage that comes of faith, we die to self
and to the way of the world. Instead, moment-by-
moment, we choose the way of God, even if it means
facing persecution.

What is the way of God? Jesus lived by it, and
encouraged his followers to do the same. He believed

that the way of God was, first and foremost, love. In the kingdom of heaven, love reigns supreme because love is the nature of God. Love becomes paramount for us and all else becomes secondary.

"Whoever does not love does not know God; for God is love." (1 John 4:8)

Because we believe in love, we dare to speak truth to power, including to governmental, religious, and corporate power.

Because we believe in love, we dare to proclaim our faith publicly.

Because we believe in love, we dare to violate civil law when it goes against divine law.

Because we believe in love, we dare to forgive transgressions, and restore lawbreakers to wholeness.

Because we believe in love, we dare to challenge religiosity and the misuse of power by ecclesiastical hierarchy.

Because we believe in love, we dare to promote social welfare, even at the cost of being judged as outsiders with intent to overthrow the status quo.

Because we believe in love, we dare to recruit followers, and promulgate love as a way of life.

To be willing to suffer in this world for the sake of love, is to be persecuted for righteousness' sake. Jesus knew well the consequence of persecution. He was not deterred, even as he walked the way of the Cross.

Dare to live according to the dictates of your heart, even in the face of persecution. Neither pain nor humiliation, neither bondage nor death, can sway you from your destiny with God.

Endings and Beginnings

Sacrifice

They had accused Jesus of stirring up the people, and of that he was guilty.

The chief priests, the elders, and the scribes conspired to arrest Jesus. They wanted him dead because the more followers he drew, the less followers they could claim. They arrested Jesus and turned him over to the Roman authorities for execution.

They had thought they were merely killing off a threat to their institutional religion. They had thought they were just removing a bothersome splinter from the side of their legalistic society. They had thought they were only eliminating one man for the sake of the nation. But what they were really doing with their false accusation, their clandestine arrest, their bogus trial, and their inhumane crucifixion, was splitting the atom of love, and causing the awesome proliferation of the Spirit of God throughout the world. They did not know that the breaking of the man would be the breaking of the bread of life that would nourish humanity for eons to come.

Jesus understood that speaking truth to power would have dire consequences. He believed his work for God was finished, and now, he had to pay the price. He knew that he must die; yet, he believed that his death would not be an ending, but a beginning. "Very truly, I tell you, unless a grain of wheat falls into the earth and dies, it remains just a single grain; but if it dies, it bears much fruit. (John 12:24)

Sacrifice is not "giving up" something held dearly; it is holding on to something held even more dearly. For Jesus, it was love that was worth even the greatest sacrifice.

For Jesus, ritual sacrifices were not what God required from human beings; it was love. When the Pharisees were rebuking Jesus and his disciples for socializing with tax collectors and sinners, Jesus quoted the prophet Hosea to them. "Go and learn what this means: 'For I desire steadfast love and not sacrifice...' (Hosea 6:6) For I have come to call not the righteous, but sinners." (Matthew 9:13)

In other words, it is from love that sacrifice emanates. If sacrifice comes of love, then surely it does not seek its own glory. It is not a tool used to manipulate the deity or a leverage over the lives of others. If sacrifice comes of love, then it has to do with going out beyond oneself in quest of a higher good.

Sacrifice compelled by love, is willing to let go of the temporal or limited good for the sake of permanent and boundless good. For sacrifice to be truly selfless and effective, one has to believe in the higher good for which the sacrifice is being made. With this higher good as the focal point of the sacrifice, the hardships that come with it can be endured; and the suffering that comes from the sacrifice is elevated and purposeful.

Jesus was not looking for a way to sacrifice; he was not wanting to be a martyr; he did not want to die. And yet, what he believed and what he taught to others threatened the powerful ecclesiastics and they demanded his annihilation. Jesus' persecutors exacted no less than the way of the cross for him.

Jesus understood Hosea well. His would not be a sacrifice to please God; but rather, a reluctant acceptance of the nature of his mission, and of its consequences.

"Now my soul is troubled. And what should I say – 'Father, save me from this hour'? No, it is for this reason that I have come to this hour." (Matthew 12:27) Later, in the Garden of Gethsemane, Jesus would pray, "Father, if it is possible, let this cup pass from me; yet not what I want but what you want." (Matthew 26:39)

Time to Say Goodbye

Fear and sadness overwhelmed Jesus as he bade farewell to those whom he loved.

Jesus' words to his disciples were solemn, "You know that after two days the Passover is coming, and the Son of Man will be handed over to be crucified." (Matthew 26:2) His words pierced their hearts. They had felt so committed to him, so enlightened by him, so united with him. Why now must the bond be broken? Why must he go away? "Where are you going?" they asked. "Jesus answered, 'Where I am going, you cannot follow me now; but you will follow afterward.'"

These men had been his disciples, his friends, his confidants. They had turned from the world to follow the young teacher wherever he might lead them. Now they would be left behind.

"Do not let your hearts be troubled." Jesus said to them, "Believe in God, believe also in me." (John 14:1) This had been his theme from the beginning: to believe in the power of God and the powerlessness of everything else. Now was the time when their faith would be tested. Now the lessons were over and reality had begun.

Jesus had given them a new way to experience life; and he modeled for them a more intimate relationship with God. He reminded them that they must follow his teachings even after they could no longer follow him.

The disciples tried to understand Jesus, but they were distraught.

"A little while, and you will no longer see me, and again a little while, and you will see me." (John 16:16) Jesus assured them that, though they be separated through death, they would forever be one in spirit.

To Jesus, death was not the end, but a transformation. He was telling his disciples that love is forever and cannot be undone, even by death. Jesus looked with compassion on the bereaved faces of those to whom he had to say goodbye. He knew they would be overcome with grief. He told them that they would be given the strength to persevere even through this tremendous loss. "Very truly I tell you, you will weep and mourn, but the world will rejoice; you will have pain, but your pain will turn into joy." (John 16:20)

But even as Jesus comforted his friends, his heart was also breaking. "Abide in me as I abide in you," he told them. (John 15:4) Especially now, Jesus wanted them to make love the center of their lives. "This is my commandment, that you love one another as I have loved you. No one has greater love than this, to lay down one's life for one's friends." (John 15:12,13)

Existential Loneliness

"I am deeply grieved, even unto death; remain here, and stay awake with me." (Matthew 26:38)

With these words, Jesus asked his closest friends to be with him in crisis; to see him through the worst chapter of his life. He asked them for compassion, comfort, and companionship.

Instead, when Jesus turned back to his friends, he found them sleeping. It was too much for them to face what was to come. They chose escape through the sleep of denial.

"So, you could not stay awake with me one hour?" (Matthew 26:40) Jesus said to them. His heart was probably sinking as he realized just how alone he was in the world. Even though Jesus was surrounded by others; in the midst of his gravest hour, their presence and their support was not offered. In his hour of extreme vulnerability and maximum danger, Jesus was all alone.

Jesus watched as his friends scattered when the confrontation with authorities became real. In this, his time of existential loneliness, he felt abandoned, empty, exposed to the wolves. There was no place else to turn but within to the secret place of his soul.

Having to let go of his reliance on others, even his loved ones, to protect him, Jesus turned to God. He had said to his friends before he was arrested, "The hour is coming, indeed it has come, when you will be scattered, each one to his home, and you will leave me alone. Yet I am not alone because the Father is with me." (John 16:32)

What human being would step up to help Jesus on his way to the Cross? Who would be strong enough, powerful enough, capable enough, to ease the burden of this innocent man?

An African man named Simon, was coming in from a hard day's work in the country, when he encountered a procession of Roman soldiers escorting Jesus toward the hill of crucifixion.

Weak from the beatings he had suffered at the hands of his captors, and faint from the loss of blood, Jesus stumbled as he carried the crossbeam of the cross to which he would soon be nailed. Simon felt compassion for the man of sorrows, but he felt helpless to do much about his plight. Suddenly, a Roman soldier ordered Simon to take the heavy crossbeam from Jesus' shoulders and carry it the rest of the way. Simon had no choice; he had to follow orders.

The Cross

Simon of Cyrene

It was a matter of being at the wrong place at the wrong time.

Or was it the right place at the right time. I am not sure anymore. In any case, it was an experience I will never forget.

My name is Simon. I was walking in from working in the fields when I heard a commotion coming from the city gates. There was a crowd of people. Some were jeering, others were wailing. I could not tell if it was another crucifixion or part of the Passover celebration. I approached to take a closer look.

My heart broke when I saw what was happening. It was a procession for a crucifixion. The soldiers were forcing a man to carry his own crossbeam through the streets. He kept falling under his heavy burden. The man was bleeding from the back as if he had been badly scourged. On his head was a crown of branches with thorns that pierced his flesh. He was weakening with every step and kept falling down. I remember feeling grateful that it was not me under that crossbeam.

I did not know what crime this man had committed, but I thought that no human being should be treated in that way. Guilty or not, cruelty is cruelty.

As I stood there helplessly watching this pitiful event, I was startled by the gruff voice of one of the soldiers. "You! Over here!" he shouted. "Pick up that crossbeam!" I was being ordered to carry the man's crossbeam. I knew I had no choice but to obey, but to myself, I protested loudly, "Why me? I am no criminal. I am tired. I just came in from working in the fields. Why not someone else? I have to get home to my two sons. They are waiting for me. I did nothing to deserve this!"

As I went to take the crossbeam from the shoulder of that wretched, broken man; he turned his head slightly and looked at me. His eyes were filled with agony. He seemed so small, so helpless, so much in need.

I lifted the crossbeam and he sighed with relief. Then someone pushed me and ordered me to move.

Halfway up the hill where he was to be crucified, they took the crossbeam from me. I left quickly, not wanting to be used anymore against my will, and not wanting to witness what was about to happen to this man. As I ran down the hill toward home, my head was still spinning in confusion and my heart was filled with many conflicting emotions.

I felt disgust at the inhumane treatment that man was enduring. I felt pity for him; he was hurting so. I felt anger at those who were so callously inflicting pain on him; and I felt powerless to do anything about it.

At first, when the soldier ordered me to help, I felt fear for myself. I felt helpless for myself. I felt anger toward those who were taking advantage of me. But when I looked into the sorrowful eyes of that man, I felt his profound pain. I was overwhelmed with compassion for him. Picking up the crossbeam and following him made me feel close to him in his last hour.

I did not even know who he was, yet, I was sharing his burden. I probably would not have volunteered to help him; yet, in retrospect, it seems so right that I did. He probably was a criminal; after all, they were going to crucify him. But to me he was still a human being, a creature of God. Why, if he was to be executed, must he also be made to suffer such excruciating torture? Is there no mercy in the law?

By helping him, I gave him a moment of relief. With his piercing eyes, he gave me a moment of profound connection that I will not forget.

Three Men, Three Crosses

Three men on three crosses, each man my brother, each man myself.

The agony of crucifixion was beyond description. In the midst of such excruciating pain and utter desperation, death became the blessing. But death did not come quickly. There was time to suffer, to think, to pray, and to despair.

Jesus was crucified between two criminals.

One man spoke bitterly from his cross. He was angry at the world for holding him accountable for his actions; he lashed out with his words at Jesus. "Are you not the Messiah? Save yourself and us." (Luke 23:39) This man had avoided responsibility all his life by fleeing from it or by blaming others for his troubles. Even now, as he reaped what he had sown, he demanded that the rules of the game be changed. He wanted the power of

Jesus to somehow save him from the suffering and death that he had brought upon himself.

The second crucified man had also lived a life of opportunism, but was more aware than the first man that he was responsible for his own life and its consequences. He rebuked the first man, "Do you not fear God, since you are under the same sentence of condemnation? And we indeed have been condemned justly, for we are getting what we deserve for our deeds, but this man has done nothing wrong."

The second crucified man believed that there was more to fear than physical suffering or even death. He feared separation from God. He feared an eternity based on the way he had lived his life. But here was his chance. He could repent. He could turn himself around, even now. He could call, not on the power of God to save his body, but on the mercy of God to save his soul. He turned to Jesus and said to him, "Jesus, remember me when you come into your kingdom." (Luke 23:40)

This man was willing to accept the suffering that had come to him because he believed he deserved it. Jesus, indeed, had done nothing wrong. He was innocent and yet suffered the same crucifixion as those who were not. How was it that he came to the Cross? He did not seek out suffering, he merely loved without reservation and spoke truth without qualification.

First, Jesus tried to avoid the suffering, but when he saw it as inevitable, he embraced it and gave it meaning for himself and others. Through his suffering, Jesus allowed himself to be transformed.

The Last Words

From the tree of torture, Jesus uttered his last words.

Jesus expressed himself amid the groans of agony and the gasps of breathlessness. Even as the soldiers drove into his flesh their nails of fear and hatred, he prayed for them. "Father, forgive them; for they do not know what they are doing." (Luke 23:34)

Jesus' prayer was love manifested in its truest form. He had made forgiveness the center point of his life and now, even as he was dying, it was still paramount to him. Letting go of even the greatest offenses is the justice of heaven; but excusing these offenses due to ignorance was a step beyond. While others were killing him slowly and methodically, this man of compassion was advocating on their behalf with God.

To the repentant man, hanging from the cross next to him, Jesus was responsive. The man had asked Jesus to remember him "when you come into your kingdom." Jesus promised him even more than he had asked for. "Truly I tell you, today you will be with me in Paradise." (Luke 23:42,43) Jesus' love went beyond forgiveness and understanding to union in God.

Even the torture of the cross, was not as painful to Jesus as the forced separation from those whom he loved. He made sure that those he left behind were going to be safe. "When Jesus saw his mother and the disciple whom he loved standing beside her, he said to his mother, 'Woman, here is your son.' Then he said to his disciple, "Here is your mother.'" (John 19:26)

Oh, what darkness was his grief! How profoundly sad to have to say goodbye. How alone and abandoned, Jesus must have felt. "My God, my God, why have you forsaken me?" (Mark 15:34)

Now was the hour of Jesus' greatest faith; not because he felt God's presence, because he did not; but because he did not sense God's love or protection, and yet believed. Such naked faith comes only through the grace of God.

It was from this place of aridity that Jesus said, "I am thirsty. (John 19:28) He was offered sour wine to drink. If even the enemy soldier was prompted by compassion to offer him something to drink, how much more would God have compassion on him. Jesus thirsted for that which only the fountain of God could quench.

Jesus had one purpose in life: to love and serve God with his total being. It was his mission to help others to realize that this was their purpose too. In his final moments, he thought about his life. He knew he had planted the seed of God's Spirit. He was confident that it would grow even through the soil of hardened hearts. His mission accomplished; his purpose fulfilled; he said, "It is finished." (John 19:30)

In the surrender of his soul, Jesus withdrew his trust from anything other than God. No king, no governor, no centurion, could save him. No sword, no band of men, no legion of angels could protect him – only God.

Jesus had lived his life in constant surrender to the will of God. He reached out his arms to heal the afflicted and to include the alienated. Now he surrendered once again as he reached out his arms to die on the Cross. Jesus prayed, "Father, into your hands I commend my spirit." (Luke 23:46)

With the intensity of all that was in him, Jesus, thrust forth one final cry that would resound into the ages. "Then Jesus cried again with a loud voice and gave up his spirit." (Matthew 27:50)

At midday, darkness fell across the land; Jesus was dead. "The light shines in the darkness, and the darkness did not overcome it." (John 1:5)

Who was this man who called himself the Son of Man; who would not be silenced even in the name of order; who was compelled by love to confront his crucifixion? Who was this man who spoke of joy from the midst of his sorrow; who triumphed over death, even as he lost his life; whose light would not be extinguished, even by the greatest darkness?

"I am the light of the world. Whoever follows me will never walk in the darkness but will have the light of life." (John 8:12)

At the Foot of the Cross

Mary's Words to Jesus

Even as I felt you in the cradle of my womb, I knew that I was blessed.

I was a humble Jewish girl with little knowledge of the world. I was in love with God, and I was receptive to God's will. It was through grace that I believed; and it was through grace that I received. I was to carry within me the seed of love, the gift that God would give the world. I did not understand, I had to turn to faith. I gave to God all that I had; God gave me you.

Blessed was the fruit of my womb, they said, and they honored you with precious gifts. All that I could give to you were swaddling clothes and a manger for a bed. You came into the world in a borrowed shelter, you would leave it just the same. Little would be yours, yet you would have so much to give. Many would exalt you, many would condemn you, but that night you were my baby, I would hold you close to me.

There were those who prophesized that you would be a king. There were those who said that you were the Messiah. I was amazed at what was said of you. I remember most of all the one who blessed you in the Temple, the one who somehow knew what was to come. "This child is destined for the falling and the rising of many in Israel...and a sword will pierce your own soul too." (Luke 2:33, 34)

As you played on my knee, I gave you all my life. I helped you and I taught you, and I cherished you each day. I wanted so to nurture you and to give you all I could. Still, I pondered in my heart all that I had heard. In the midst of the joy I felt when I held you in my arms, I felt a sadness deep within that I did not understand.

As you grew in mind and stature, I marveled in your being. Once I thought you had been lost, and I nearly lost my mind. Then I found you in the Temple teaching and learning, oblivious to my pain. My anger toward you faded next to my joy of finding you.

Suddenly, you were a man with a mission of your own. Sometimes you would leave for days to go and be alone. Sometimes you would sit and talk to people for hours at a time. You seemed to enjoy the company of friends; yet, there were times when you went into the desert for repose and solitude.

Others began to follow you. You had so much to say. You seemed alive and full of energy when you talked about your God. But even then, you were frustrated when you were misunderstood.

Your mission grew beyond what I expected. You touched others in such special ways. There was healing in your presence; there was enlightenment in your words. You were salve for the wounded, and inspiration for the lost. You reflected the glory of God; yet, I felt such fear for you. As your influence grew, so did the jealousy of those who were threatened by your popularity. They could not let you be without losing their credibility. The tide began to turn against you.

I had tended you when you were sick, and held you when you were afraid. I kissed your little finger when you hurt it, and I protected you from any harm. Now, I was powerless. Now, I could not intervene. It seemed no one could deter you from what you had to do. I cried, I prayed, I stood by helplessly.

Then, they came to tell me you had been arrested. Then, they told me you had been tried. There were stories back and forth. I was confused. Then, it happened. You were sentenced to be killed. The sword that was to pierce my soul had come as prophesized.

I begged them to take me to the Place of the Skull. There, I entered into hell. What agony! What terror in my heart! Dear Jesus! What are they doing to my son? Please don't hurt him! Please release him! Please don't let him die! His blood is innocent. His love is pure. My pleas were all in vain.

I, who cared for you your whole life through, now looked on as they tortured you upon that cross. I, who had suckled you with my sweet milk, now watched them wet your lips with sour wine. I, who had formed you in my womb, now witnessed your destruction.

Even in your torment, you talked with God. Even as you were dying, you tended to my needs. You looked at me with painful, loving eyes and commended me to the one you trusted. You prayed once more, then you were gone. The gift of love God gave to me, I released unto the ages. Though your flesh be torn from me, my son, your spirit will forever grace my heart. Goodbye my precious son, goodbye my everything.

The Centurion

I was there.

I was a Roman soldier, a centurion assigned to the headquarters of Governor Pontius Pilate of Judea. I was part of the Roman Imperial System that kept order among the Jews and carried out the crucifixions. This torturous method of execution was supposed to deter the breaking of Roman law.

All the crucifixions in which I participated were cruel and merciless, but this particular crucifixion has tortured my soul since the day it happened.

The crucified was a man from Nazareth, who had already been exonerated by the governor of the charges brought against him by the Temple authorities. Yet, political pressure was exerted on the governor to crucify the Nazarene, guilty or not.

I was there when the governor interrogated him. Strangely, the Nazarene did not defend himself. He was a pitiful sight as he stood there allowing this gross injustice to run its course.

To please the jeering crowd, the governor had the Nazarene flogged. I was there, but I did not stop the hideous abuse of the prisoner. The other soldiers enjoyed themselves mocking him, spitting on him, and stripping him of his clothing. They put a robe on him and a crown of thorns and called him, "King of the Jews."

The flogging did not satisfy the crowd. The protesters wanted death by crucifixion and nothing less. So, the governor ordered the Nazarene to be crucified, even as he washed his hands, and declared himself innocent of the murder that was about to happen.

I was there as we walked the Nazarene to his death. He was weak from lack of sleep and from the bloody beating he had undergone. I was aware of how difficult it was for him to carry the crossbeam of his cross, so I conscripted a passerby to carry the crossbeam for him. It was the least that I could do.

I was there when we nailed the Nazarene to his cross. I had pounded nails at other crucifixions, but I could not do it at this one. I could not do it, but I was the one who ordered it done. Why inflict such excruciating pain on an innocent man, or on any man? It took so long to die.

I was there when the soldiers divided among themselves the Nazarene's clothing. But then there was the question of his robe. It was seamless and could not be torn apart. We cast lots for it. I won it. I took it. I would have a piece of him.

I had never felt guilt conducting crucifixions before. Why then was my heart filled with guilt and remorse? And then, I heard the Nazarene pray from his cross, "Father, forgive them; for they do not know what they are doing. (Luke 23:34) How could he plead to God for our forgiveness, even as we were killing him? Though he forgave me; though God forgave me; I would never forgive myself.

The Nazarene cried out then took his last breath. He was dead. One of my soldiers pierced his side to make sure he was dead. When I saw the blood and water drain from his wound, I said to the others, "Certainly, this man was innocent." (Luke 23:47)

Joseph of Arimathea

Only in the obscurity of the night or the anonymity of the crowd had Joseph of Arimathea met with Jesus.

Although a disciple of Jesus, associating with him openly was not a prudent thing to do for a man who belonged to the Sanhedrin, the Great Council of the Jews. How would it look for a respected person of the Jewish faith to have dealings with this "blasphemer?"

Joseph had been careful because, although he had experienced something unusual in his heart when he had met with Jesus, he feared he had too much to lose by openly declaring his interest in him.

The Spirit that moved within Joseph had given him the strength to resist being swept up along with the rest of the Sanhedrin in opposition to Jesus' ministry. Joseph, in fact, had abstained from the proceedings that judged the controversial Galilean.

Why now, when Jesus was already dead on the cross, when Joseph had apparently nothing to gain, did he openly declare himself as a disciple of Jesus? He could have kept his friendship with Jesus secret. He could have joined the other frightened disciples who were in hiding until it was safe. He could have just stayed silent and allowed the birds and dogs to eat the flesh off the corpse of Jesus.

Instead, the middle-aged man of high position and substantial wealth risked all that he had treasured. He went boldly to ask permission from Pilate the governor to take the body of Jesus down from the Cross before the time it was normally allowed, and had him buried in a tomb that he owned.

In the ways of the world, Joseph of Arimathea had much to lose by aligning himself with Jesus. At some point, however, he discovered that, in reality, he had nothing to lose and everything to gain by being true to his most inward beliefs. Joseph of Arimathea was true to his faith when it really counted.

Eye Witness

I was fascinated by the stories I had heard about a young revolutionary they called Jesus, so I traveled from my home in Damascus to Jerusalem to see for myself what the commotion was all about.

Although this territory is Roman-occupied, traveling about was allowed.

While Jesus was hard to find, I finally managed to locate him and to observe him as he talked with the large groups that followed him. I also talked with some men and women who knew him personally.

I was told that Jesus, who came from Galilee to the north, was a soft, meek, patient, humble, tranquil spirit. They told me that on a one-to-one basis he was peaceful and warm, and that he was the first true gentleman they had ever known.

My experience was different from what I had been told. This was not a man of soft, patient, and tranquil spirit that those crowds were coming to hear. This man was followed because he was exciting, uncompromising, stormy, and formidable. His words were packed with energy. He was vehement, vigorous, exuberant, and even extravagant.

Jesus was in his early 30's, but he seemed to have lived a full life and related his experiences vividly. When he spoke, one could see men straining out gnats and swallowing camels, men with logs in their eyes, and others cutting off their hands to escape worse consequences.

Jesus used strong language, but he seemed earnest. It was obvious that he did not intend for his words be taken literally, but metaphorically. He seemed to know himself well, and also those to whom he spoke. Although he was dynamic, his homelier qualities and his ability to be at ease with all sorts of people, drew the common folk to him. I think this is what stirred the Temple authorities into such an uproar.

Once, I heard him speaking to a group of Temple authorities. He was angry at them and called them hypocrites, blind guides, and whitewashed tombs full of rotten things. He accused them of teaching legalisms instead of justice, mercy, and honesty. Then he walked up the mountain with a small group of men who seemed to follow him everywhere.

The Temple authorities were already against Jesus. He did not need to say those things to them. They had already accused him of feeding his belly and that of his friends with wheat picked from the fields on the Sabbath. They said he put hunger above the laws of the Temple.

Others in the community called him a miracle worker, a magician, supernatural, not human. He told his followers that they too could perform the healings that they witnessed him doing. He told them they could be as gods.

Jesus claimed that he was totally dependent on God for all he said and did, and that he merely listened to God and obeyed God's will.

Jesus seemed pretty human to me. The way that he held that child on his lap that day; the way he spoke to her and looked into her eyes; that overwhelming love was very real. One day, I witnessed him weeping. These were tears of pain, tears of sadness, tears from a broken heart for a friend who had died. They were human tears.

Jesus traveled the area extensively and many people were getting to know him. He talked about a lot of things, but mostly about living and loving. He spoke about reality. He talked about the clear vision he had of God.

When I first came looking for Jesus, I thought I would find him riling up the masses with revolutionary slogans and speeches about the plight of the oppressed. Instead, I found a serious, down-to-earth man, comforting others in their grief; healing the sick, using their own faith to do it; and promoting loving-kindness. I came to witness a political rebellion; instead, I found a spiritual revolution.

Some of his followers told me that Jesus had come from God. But if that were true, why did he allow those Roman soldiers to ridicule him and push him around? Why did he allow the Roman governor to have him whipped until he fell into bloody unconsciousness? Why didn't he use the power of God to help himself? Why, if he really came from God, did he let them nail him to a cross, to pierce his body, to torture him, and to kill him?

At the place where they crucified Jesus, I met a man named John, who claimed to be a disciple. He told me that Jesus had indeed come from God and that he had been sent to call humanity to God. He said that it was out of love that Jesus had chosen the way of the Cross – the way of humiliation and total renunciation of power. John told me that his Master's death was the not the end for him, but the beginning of new life.

I didn't get it. How could weakness be strength? How could powerlessness be power? How could death be life?

Only a few followers were left at the foot of the cross, including a woman kneeling, sobbing, and shaking with grief. I approached her. She looked up at me through her tears. "They have killed my son," she said, then collapsed at the foot of the cross. John was there for her, though she would not be consoled.

I turned and descended the mount. I had not known the man, and yet, my heart was sorrowful.

The life of Jesus had come to a tragic end. Now it remained to be seen what, if any, would be the effect of his life and of his death.

The Spirit

The Light of the World

What has come into being in him was life, and the life was the light of all people. (John 1:4)

For a while it seemed that the mission of Jesus had failed.

Mary, the mother of Jesus and her sister were at the foot of the Cross, as were Mary Magdalene and John, the disciple whom Jesus loved. But where were the others whom Jesus had called friends? They had scattered, frightened for their own lives, and grievous not only for the death of Jesus, but also of the expectations they had of his life.

What happened to these friends of Jesus soon afterward cannot be adequately explained. Here were men and women abandoning him in his greatest need, denying him, doubting him, not understanding him, and even giving up hope on him. Yet, suddenly, something miraculous happened to them after Jesus' death that radically changed them, and, consequently, affected the world forever.

Where before, they had cowered in their hiding places, waiting for the danger to recede, they now had the courage to speak for Jesus even in the face of danger. They believed in him, lived in him, and remained true to him even unto death.

What had happened to these sheep-turned-into-lions? What happened that converted their fear into energy, persecution into challenge, and tragedy into love? Some say that they saw Jesus again, and that they spoke to him, walked with him, and ate with him. Somehow, these men and women were closer to Jesus in spirit than they had been in person.

Some say that the disciples were gathered on a mountain when they experienced the presence of Jesus' spirit. It is said that they heard the voice of his holy spirit instructing them to carry on his ministry throughout the world and reminding them, "I am with you always, to the end of the age." (Matthew 28:16-20)

Living our Faith

We too are seeking congruence between what we have come to believe and what we are ready to live.

After the blood of Friday, and the tears of Saturday, comes the joy of Sunday. Then the hardest part comes – getting on with life on Monday.

Jesus repeatedly asked Peter, "Do you love me?" Peter repeatedly responded, "Yes, Lord; you know that I love you." Jesus said, "Tend my sheep." (John 21: 15) Declaring our love for Jesus is important, but our love becomes real only when we demonstrate it through our life.

When Jesus saw the crowds, he had compassion for them, because they were harassed and helpless, like sheep without a shepherd. Then he said to his disciples, "The harvest is plentiful, but the laborers are few; therefore, ask the Lord of the harvest to send out laborers into his harvest." (Matthew 9:36) Jesus' disciples understood his metaphor. The Lord of the harvest was God, and they were the laborers sent by God.

Jesus instructed his twelve apostles, "As you go, proclaim the good news, 'The kingdom of heaven is at hand.' Cure the sick, raise the dead, cleanse the lepers, cast out demons." (Matthew 10:7) In the same way, we are sent out by the spirit of God to tend our fellow human beings.

We proclaim the kingdom of heaven. We tell the people that God is as close to them as their hearts; and that God calls all of us into union with one another.

We cure the sick. We have the power to bring others to wholeness through love. We reach out not only to those who are physically ill, but to those who are emotionally and spiritually broken.

We raise the dead. We call to life those who have died to the glory that is humanity. We spark in them a motivation to live abundantly. We lead them to the resurrection of hope and the adventure of faith.

We cleanse the lepers. We bring into the fold those who have been discarded by society; we take the hand of the dejected; we wash their feet, and ask their forgiveness on behalf of the world.

We cast out devils. We show to those who follow us the power of God's love and the powerlessness of everything else.

The Spirit is Upon Us

For this I was born," said Jesus, "and for this I came into the world, to testify to the truth. (John 8:37)

Jesus knew exactly what his mission was. In the synagogue he read from Isaiah: 'The Spirit of the Lord is upon me, because he has anointed me to bring good news to the poor. He has sent me to proclaim release to the captives and recovery of sight to the blind, to let the oppressed go free, to proclaim the year of the Lord's favor." (Luke 4:14-19)

The Spirit of God is upon each one of us as well. It has come into our heart and will live and move and act from there if we allow it. We are all God's chosen ones, and we have been anointed to preach the Gospel to the poor. Who are the poor? They are the ones who find themselves alienated from life, lonely, and empty-handed. The persons who feel abandoned, hopeless, and unloved are the poor. Whether economically, emotionally, or spiritually poor, we are here to respond to them with all that God has given us.

Preaching the Gospel does not necessarily mean evangelizing with words, although it certainly includes this. It also means living out the Gospel message of love before others. The Gospel that we preach has to do with God's unconditional and inalienable relationship with us. God sends us out into a hard and unkind world to do love's bidding. God asks that we touch our fellow human beings, and let them know God loves them.

God has sent us to heal the brokenhearted. We, who have not been spared the pain that comes with living, are given the power to heal others through compassionate action. It seems only the broken can truly minister unto the broken. The healing comes, not from any spiritual magic, but from the warm and gentle treatment we offer to others. Through our care and understanding, hearts mend and tears are wiped away. By being there to listen and encourage, the balance of the soul is restored.

We are sent to preach deliverance to the captives. First, we must free ourselves from the ties that bind us to our lesser selves, then we can help others to also break away. We are all captives of something. Some of us are caught in the web of our addictions. Some of us are chained to a destructive way of life. Others of us are prisoners of our memories. The Spirit moving through us can deliver us and others from all that is not of God.

We are sent to offer sight to the blind. Because we too have been blind, we know the terror of the darkness. We know that the only hope for light is through unceasing prayer and contemplation.

We are sent to love one another in such a way that the scales of fear and prejudice fall away from our eyes. Through the sharing of the love of God, we are able to share with each other a spiritual view that we cannot see with our physical eyes. As we carry love into the world, we carry the light that overcomes the darkness.

We are sent to set at liberty those who are oppressed. Through our closeness with God, we can help others to stand up for themselves and to be free. We are the mercy of God that forgives others so that they may be liberated from their debts and wrongdoings. We are the compassion of God that alleviates the inhuman conditions under which many live and die.

"Truly I tell you, just as you did it to one of the least of these who are members of my family, you did it to me." (Matthew 25:40)

Also by Adolfo Quezada

A Grief Revisited

Old Soul, Young Spirit

Praying to an Unknown God

Before the Night Comes

Love is My Religion

Return to Silence

Teaching Minds, Touching Hearts

A Spiritual Soliloquy

Spirit of Repose

Attention: A Gift of Love

Passages of Faith

My Soul in Winter

Adolfo Quezada is a retired counselor and psychotherapist. He lives in Tucson, Arizona.